I Serve at God's Altar

THE MINISTRY OF ACOLYTES

Roger A. Speer Jr. and Sharon Ely Pearson

CHURCH
PUBLISHING
INCORPORATED

Dedication

In loving memory of the Reverend Larry Jackson, my first acolyte master, and in grateful thanksgiving for the life and ministry of the Reverend Robert Fain, my current one. —Roger

In thanksgiving for all the acolytes at St. Matthew's Episcopal Church in Wilton, Connecticut. —Sharon

Church Publishing
19 East 34th Street
New York, NY 10016
www.churchpublishing.org

Cover art by Roger A. Speer Jr.

Cover design by Jennifer Kopec, 2Pug Design
Typeset by Rose Design

Library of Congress Cataloging-in-Publication Data

Names: Speer, Roger A., Jr., author.
Title: I serve at God's altar : the ministry of acolytes / Roger A. Speer
  Jr., Sharon Ely Pearson.
Description: New York : Church Publishing, 2018. | Includes bibliographical
  references.
Identifiers: LCCN 2018028366 (print) | LCCN 2018036307 (ebook) | ISBN
  9781640651241 (ebook) | ISBN 9781640651234 (pbk.)
Subjects: LCSH: Acolytes--Episcopal Church.
Classification: LCC BX5948 (ebook) | LCC BX5948 .S64 2018 (print) | DDC
  264/.03--dc23
LC record available at https://lccn.loc.gov/2018028366

Printed in the United States of America

Contents

Making This Work

The Ministry of the Acolyte

Crafting Your Way of Life

Crafting Your Program Mission Statement

Mapping Out Your Choreography

Administrative Helps

A Sample Acolyte Retreat

A Guided Eucharist

A Visual Tour Guide

The Choreography of Processions

Church Manners for Acolytes

Your Preworship Checklist

Movements and Standards

Censing and Bell Ringing

The Holy Eucharist (Poster)

Debriefing Your Service

Commissioning Service

An Order of Worship Game

Acolyte Prayers

Introduction

IN THE ANCIENT CHURCH, as it continues today, the ministers of the church are those who have been baptized: laypersons, bishops, priests, and deacons. Some within the order of the laity are called to undertake ministries that are just as integral to worship as those who are ordained. These liturgical ministers are not "roles" in the theatrical sense because the liturgy is not a stage production, but a "work of the people." All the ministers (lay or ordained) serve the worshiping assembly, and in so doing, they serve God. In serving at God's altar, we also serve God's people.

Despite the changing landscape of our churches' membership, one worship-based ministry that continues but gets little attention is that of the acolyte. Whether they are second graders or adults, the ministry of an acolyte could be one of *the* formational experiences individuals have in the Episcopal Church. Whether it is a typical Sunday Eucharist, a marriage, baptism, funeral, or other worship service, an acolyte's work and presence is a gift to God.

A LITTLE HISTORY

The word *acolyte* is derived from the Greek word *akolouthos*, meaning companion, follower, attendant, or helper. This ministry has its roots in the Hebrew Scriptures, where the prophet Samuel is seen assisting Eli, the Levite priest, and Elisha is seen assisting Elijah the Prophet. In the early church, we might think of those who carried the light into the dark catacombs, leading others who gathered to worship as the first Christian acolytes.

Mentioned as a minor order (a transitory step leading to a "major" order such as deacon, priest, or bishop) beginning in the third century, acolytes assisted deacons at the preparation of the table. The first written historical record of the term *acolyte* appears in a letter from Pope Cornelius to the bishop of Antioch in 251 CE. In his letter, the pope lists the clergy of Rome, which included forty-two acolytes.[1] According to the ancient discipline of the Roman Church, the order of acolyte was conferred as the candidate approached adolescence, about the age of twenty, as the decree of Pope Siricius (385) to Himerius, bishop of Tarragonia in Spain, was written. In ancient ecclesiastic Rome, there was no solemn ordination of acolytes. At communion time in any ordinary Mass, the candidate approached the pope, or in his absence, one of the bishops of the pontifical court. At an earlier moment of the Mass, the acolyte had been vested with a stole and chasuble. Holding in his arms a linen bag carrying the consecrated hosts, he prostrated himself (lay facedown on the ground) while the pontiff pronounced over him a simple blessing before he carried fragments of the bread consecrated at the papal Mass to other churches.

Between the fifth and ninth centuries, the *Ordines Romani*, a series of ancient directions to the clergy, described acolyte duties that included leading processions preceding the pope as well as carrying candles to accompany the reader of the Gospel to ensure that he had enough light to read the text. In Gaul about the year 500, the candidate for acolyte was first instructed by the bishop in the duties of his office, and then a candlestick, with a candle extinguished, was placed in his hand by the archdeacon, as a sign that the lights of the church would be in his care; moreover, an empty cruet was given to him, symbolic of his office of presenting wine and water at the altar for the holy sacrifice. A short blessing followed. Acolytes were unknown outside Rome and North Africa until the tenth century, when they were introduced throughout the Western Church.

The Council of Trent (1545–63) defined the order and hoped to reactivate it on the pastoral level, but it became only a preparatory rite, or minor order, leading to the priesthood. The history of acolytes becomes confused as churches in Europe broke away from the Church of Rome, including when England's Henry VIII split the English Church in 1531, forming the Anglican Church of England. After the Reformation, many of these duties were taken over by lay clerks; in the late Middle Ages, when candles began to appear upon altars, they lighted the altar candles.

Eventually lay servers (sacristans) performed these duties as part of their training for the priesthood. Later in the nineteenth century, the clerks were suppressed and their duties were largely taken over by lay "acolytes" and sacristans or altar guilds, who did not serve at the altar but "behind the scenes" in helping to prepare the vessels and other paraphernalia for worship. During the Oxford movement in the 1830s, the Anglican Church, including the Episcopal Church, slowly returned to more traditional practices, and the ministry of acolytes

---

1. Donna H. Barthle. *Acolyte Leader's Resource Guide* (Harrisburg, PA: Morehouse Publishing, 2003), 1.

began to appear again in non-Roman churches. It wasn't until the late 1970s that girls and women were admitted to this all male ministry in the Episcopal Church. It should also be noted that it wasn't until January 1973 that Pope Paul VI decreed that the office of acolyte should no longer be called a minor order and that it should be open to laymen (in the Roman Catholic Church).

WHO ARE THE ACOLYTES TODAY?

Acolytes come in all shapes and sizes, and many churches encourage young people to take on these roles. Howard Galley wrote in 1989: "From the beginning, and for centuries afterward, the liturgical ministry of acolytes was an adult ministry. Today in contrast, it is largely a ministry of children and adolescents."[2] He then went on to question the tendency to restrict this ministry to young people alone, desiring that this ministry be encouraged for lay adults as well. We acknowledge this is a ministry for all ages; eucharistic ministers often serve as acolytes today and it would behoove those trained in that role to also be trained in acolyte ministry.

In preparing this book, we conducted a survey to learn more about the ministry of acolytes in our (Episcopal) congregations. Is there an average age? How are they trained? What roles do they take in worship?

We learned that there is a universal role of acolytes in Episcopal liturgy as well as diverse practices. Large congregations have a cadre of teams who serve; small congregations have a handful of adults with a couple of children. Fifty percent of those who responded to our survey have between five and ten acolytes involved in worship services. Ninety percent of acolytes serve as crucifers and torchbearers, light and extinguish candles, assist the clergy at the altar, offer the lavabo bowl, carry alms basins, and carry the Gospel Book in procession. Other roles include serving as a thurifer, boat bearer, or banner bearer, and ringing the Sanctus bells.

Acolytes often take the role of the bishop's chaplain during episcopal visitations. Other roles in much smaller numbers include refilling chalices, packing communion kits, carrying flags, and closing the altar rail. Reflecting the diversity of the vestments (and piety) worn in our churches, 66 percent of acolytes wear albs and cinctures, while the remaining 34 percent wear cassock and cotta. Most acolytes began their ministry when they were between ten and twelve years old.

Today, we see acolytes dressed in robes of red or white, quietly carrying torches, crosses, alms basins, and cruets. A vital part of worship, they blend into the background, helping our liturgies flow smoothly. We may see them hold the altar book open before the presider at the Eucharist or bear the Gospel Book in procession and at the proclamation; they may carry the vessels to the

---

2. Howard E. Galley, *The Ceremonies of the Eucharist: A Guide to Celebration* (Cambridge, MA: Cowley Publications, 1989), 34.

Lord's Table, wash the presider's hands (*lavabo*), bring additional vessels to the altar after the consecration of the bread and wine, or clear the altar after communion. When carrying a processional cross, they are known as the crucifer; called a thurifer when swinging the incense pot.

It would seem the ancient tradition is still alive and well in our churches today.

ABOUT THIS BOOK

We offer a simplified theology of how God is met in worship and how that affects the acolyte's discernment for ministry as well as a way of life. We also explore how to form empowered acolytes that bond together, grow together, and support each other—a model of Christian service and community. And yes, the practical stuff such as how to light the candles and carry the cross are included in our tips for training and mentoring, along with an extensive glossary and appendix that is full of illustrated handouts.

We have designed this book for the acolyte mentor—clergy or lay—who is called to walk alongside young people as well as other adults in learning what it means to actively serve God in a holy setting. We know that there is not one book that can reflect the various procedures, spaces, and "tools of the trade" found in every Episcopal congregation. Vestments and styles of worship differ from church to church; hopefully you will find your church's practices among these pages—whether you are liturgically broad, Anglo-Catholic, use a veiled chalice and incense, or have a praise band. Adapt what you find to fit your own circumstances. You may choose to give this book to each acolyte, or you may duplicate the pages found in the appendix for use in your trainings.

OUR PRAYER

The ministry of an acolyte is built upon a formative system of development that is changeless, consistent, powerful, and transformative. We seek to reclaim the role of acolyte as a religious seeker, a minor order of the church rooted in discernment that will lift up this vital, yet quiet, ministry in our worship settings. We hope that the information, engaging illustrations, and outlines that are provided within these pages assist in lifting up the ministry of acolytes in our congregations as well as empowering those called to this ministry. May each of us embrace what we learn as we serve God as a way of life that will stay with us forever.

> Let love be genuine; hate what is evil, hold fast to what is good; love one another with mutual affection; outdo one another in showing honor. Do not lag in zeal, be ardent in spirit, serve the Lord. Rejoice in hope, be patient in suffering, persevere in prayer. (Rom. 12:9–12)

ROGER A. SPEER JR.
SHARON ELY PEARSON
The Feast of Pentecost, 2018

CHAPTER ONE

A New Order

Q. Who are the ministers of the Church?

A. The ministers of the Church are lay persons, bishops, priests, and deacons.

Q. What is the ministry of the laity?

A. The ministry of lay persons is to represent Christ and his Church; to bear witness to him wherever they may be; and, according to the gifts given them, to carry on Christ's work of reconciliation in the world; and to take their place in the life, worship, and governance of the Church. (Book of Common Prayer, 855)

TO BE AN ACOLYTE IS ONE MEANS by which children, youth, and adults can take their place in the life, worship, and governance of the Church. By virtue of the sacrament of Holy Baptism, all are full members of the Church. With "membership" comes responsibility, and for the Church this involves participating in God's mission of restoration and reconciliation. This is accomplished through prayer, worship, proclaiming the gospel, and promoting justice, peace, and love in living out our Baptismal Covenant. Striving to achieve these promises is a challenging and lifelong calling for every Christian. Being an acolyte opens the door to explore one's gifts and discern where God may be calling one to serve, the experience of serving at God's altar can provide the tools of awareness, calmness, servanthood, and prayer that can last a lifetime.

As noted in the introduction, at one point in time of the history of the Church, to be an acolyte was to be part of one of the minor orders of the Church. While at the time this was most likely one of the steps toward ordination to the priesthood, today it can be seen as a means to which a person learns what service is about and what it means to serve God. What if we reclaimed the role of acolyte as a religious seeker, and rebranded the ministry of acolytes as one model of discernment? This could include discernment toward ordination, but also discernment to embrace one's place in the priesthood of all believers.

Former Presiding Bishop Frank T. Griswold describes it well:

> The Episcopal Church is a liturgical church. Through ordered worship we open ourselves to the deep, sometimes dangerous possibility of being met by Christ. Through such an encounter we find that our lives are no longer our own. We have been cracked open and caught up in the ever unfolding of Christ's presence—Christ's continuing work of healing and reconciliation—in our own day and time.
>
> Worship needs to be approached on the tiptoe of expectation. We need always to be open to its capacity to surprise and illumine us with the presence of Christ—the Lion of the tribe of Judah—who is always ready to pounce, paws first, into our lives.[3]

BEING FORMED BY THE LITURGY

Acolytes are formed by liturgy and the repetition of being a server, torchbearer, crucifer, thurifer, or any other participatory role in worship over time. "Sacramental worship requires repetition because grace is developmental over time."[4] If this ministry is seen as a chore, it is more difficult to internalize. As a practice, it can form a foundation for a new life of prayer. Metaphorically, our spiritual lives are formed like a potter who turns a hunk of clay into a piece of art. As the clay is spun on a wheel and shaped by hands rolling up and down, inside and out, it begins to take the shape of the potter's imagination, forming a new creation. It is not an easy process, and oftentimes the shape falls in upon itself or needs to be pounded back down to start again. So it is with prayer and our openness to allow worship mold us into what the Spirit would have us become—a vessel of God's love.

Learning how to be an expert potter takes practice. So it is with worship and learning what it means to be an acolyte: repetition and practice of following the ebb and flow of the liturgy helps all of us—young and old, lay and ordained—be formed in the mind of Christ. Sometimes our youth (and those older) find the traditions of the Church to be archaic and out of touch with today's world. Some might feel going to church is part of one's weekly routine, a chore that has to be done. Worship is not a routine, but a ritual. Our prayers and liturgies have been fashioned and created over long periods of time

---

3. Frank T. Griswold, "A Message from the Presiding Bishop," in *Liturgy as Formation* (New York: Domestic and Foreign Missionary Society, 2003), 4.

4. Ibid.

throughout the ages. Bishop Neil Alexander, currently dean and president of the Seminary of the South in Sewanee, Tennessee, delineates between the two:

> A routine is an oft-repeated chore that simply has to be done with some frequency. It's not particularly fulfilling and if it were possible not to, the doing of it would not be missed. . . . A ritual is quite different. Rituals depend upon frequent repetition and sometimes they too can feel like a chore. When we fail to keep our rituals, however, be they personal or religious, we feel disoriented and disconnected.[5]

We learn by doing, and this includes learning how to be an acolyte. Like the clay, those who serve at God's altar (and we could also say those in the congregation) are shaped and reshaped, formed and transformed, by our willingness to be open to God's call in our active participation in the patterns and rituals of our worship.

ACOLYTES AND DISCERNMENT

For many who serve as acolytes, their choice to "join the ranks" may have come by personal invitation from a clergyperson or mentor, part of a confirmation requirement, or simply by being that warm body who consistently showed up and was asked if they would be willing to carry a cross or light the candles. What if the invitation to serve as an acolyte—whether as a young person or adult—was rephrased: "How is God calling you to serve?" As Paul wrote to the Corinthians, "However that may be, let each of you lead the life that the Lord has assigned, to which God called you. This is my rule in all the churches" (1 Cor. 7:17).

God calls each of us. There are a variety of calls, and no one call is inherently better or higher than any other. *Call* can be used interchangeably with the word *vocation*, which comes from the Latin word *vocare*, "to call." *Vocation* has a broad connotation, while *call* may refer to something specific. Suzanne Farnham and others state, "As our lives become more centered in God, we tend to grow in our sense that God touches others through our work, whatever that work may be."[6] A "call" usually involves service or a benefit to others. As stated in the opening excerpt of this chapter taken from the Book of Common Prayer, all Christians are called to minister both to one another and to those around them by participating in God's work in the world. The difference between simply volunteering or doing work and discerning and answering a call is a mutual action with the recognition that it is God at the center of what we do and why we are doing it. In all duties, whether

5. J. Neil Alexander, "Liturgical Pottery: On the Shape of Formation," in *Liturgy as Formation* (New York: Domestic and Foreign Missionary Society, 2003), 82.

6. Suzanne G. Farnham, Joseph P. Gill, R. Taylor McLean, and Susan M. Ward, *Listening Hearts: Discerning Call in Community*, rev. ed. (Harrisburg, PA: Morehouse, 1991), 107.

formal or informal, acolytes are a reminder to us all that through our baptism we are all called to live a life of service.

The authors of *Listening Hearts* name specific ways to prepare to hear God's call.[7] What if we were to focus on these steps in our invitation to those who are interested in becoming an acolyte? What if we reinforced and mentored those who are already serving in this capacity to see their ministry through the eyes of discernment?

Trust

Acolytes learn their roles and responsibilities, trusting that the liturgy is the work of the people and they do not need to know it all or do it all. Together, those who serve at God's altar work together, following the ebb and flow of worship. While pieces of the service may change from time to time, there is comfort in being able to trust in God's presence at all times—and mistakes happen. Trusting in the forgiveness of God as well as the knowledge that one is never alone at God's altar is an example of how throughout our whole lives we can "put our trust in the Lord." This may take time and experience as one grows in confidence, but it comes.

Listening

Being an acolyte means listening to the rhythm of the liturgy. It is a somewhat silent call, as acolytes do not need to speak at all while serving. It is all about paying attention, following the ebb and flow of prayer, hymnody, and scripture being read. Each piece of the dance of worship has a meaning, and each often has an action associated with it: standing to sing, bowing one's head during prayer, holding a torch still while the Gospel is proclaimed. While listening during worship perhaps the Word of God is recognized in a new, more personal way while the acolyte is serving.

Prayer

Before worship it is typical that all who are vested and ready to serve at God's altar gather for prayer. This may be done in the sacristy or hurriedly as everyone lines up for the procession. It is just the beginning. Throughout the liturgy, moments of silence in prayer and listening offer opportunities to ponder where God is acting—in one's own life as well as the community gathered.

Knowledge of Scripture

Those who serve and worship on a regular basis come to know the story of God's people. One does not need to be a biblical scholar to discover the themes of creation, sin, judgement, reconciliation, redemption, and love found throughout the stories shared in our lectionary and prayers.

Humility

An acolyte is humble by virtue of the ministry itself. Basically, acolytes are like good waiters

---

7. *The Listening Hearts* program notes each of the following seven ways one might use to prepare to hear God's call (pages 29–37). Here we take these points and apply them to the ministry of acolytes and how each is needed for this ministry and how each may help the individual discern where God may be calling them to a more holistic way of life.

who tend to all the details of a meal, often quietly working without being noticed at all. Being attentive to the needs of others, whether it be supplying the celebrant with the necessary implements or making sure a minister of communion has enough wine in their chalice, an acolyte is always at the ready to serve in humble silence.

Patience and Urgency

Sometimes it is like hurry, hurry, hurry, only to have to wait. Arrive early, vest, and light the candles. Then wait for that long prelude to conclude. Walk slowly in procession, but not so slow as the choir member behind you may bump against your heels. Watch and wait to enact your next responsibility, but when the time comes, move quickly and accomplish the task. Like waiting for God, being ready at a moment's notice is the ministry of an acolyte.

Perspective

Being an acolyte is being part of a team. All players are important. And while each may know something about the role to be played, no one is probably capable of filling all the roles. And

from a congregational perspective, most are clueless as to what the acolyte is doing—which means they are doing their job perfectly.

A New Order for Today's World

The Church recognizes three ordained orders today: bishops, priests, and deacons. In the early Church, four minor orders were also ordained: acolytes, lectors, exorcists, and *ostiarii* (known today as vergers).[8] These early acolytes had functions very similar to those of today—they were to assist the bishop and clergy during liturgical services and help lead and define the tone of worship for the community.

The early acolytes gave strong witness to their Christian faith and were dedicated to their worship community. Tarsicus, an acolyte in Rome, was martyred in 258 when he was found bringing the Eucharist to those who were unable to attend worship. St. Vincent of Saragossa, the patron saint of acolytes, was a deacon who was martyred in 304 CE, now commemorated on the calendar on January 22. Vincent is remembered for his love of God, his faithfulness to his bishop, his unswerving loyalty to his responsibilities, and for his defense of Christianity in a Roman

---

8. "And whereas the ministry of so holy a priesthood is a divine thing; to the end that it might be exercised in a more worthy manner, and with greater veneration, it was suitable that, in the most well-ordered settlement of the church, there should be several and diverse orders of ministers, to minister to the priesthood, by virtue of their office; orders so distributed as that those already marked with the clerical tonsure should ascend through the lesser to the greater orders. For the sacred Scriptures make open mention not only of priests, but also of deacons; and teach, in words the most weighty, what things are especially to be attended to in the Ordination thereof; and, from the very beginning of the church, the names of the following orders, and the ministrations proper to each one of them, are known to have been in use; to wit those of subdeacon, acolyte, exorcist, lector, and door-keeper; though these were not of equal rank: for the subdeaconship is classed amongst the greater orders by the Fathers and sacred Councils, wherein also we very often read of the other inferior orders." From "Chapter II. On the Seven Orders" in *Doctrine on the Sacrament of Ordination* (The Fourth Session of The Council of Trent, July 15, 1563), accessed February 20, 2018, *http://www.thecounciloftrent.com/ch23.htm*.

court. Throughout the centuries, acolytes continue to be dedicated witnesses for Christ in both dramatic and mundane ways, witnessing to a piece of our apostolic tradition that spans at least seventeen centuries.

While these early Church acolytes may have been on a path toward ordination[9] in one of the three major orders of the time, today's acolyte in the Episcopal Church may not be on that path but on another one, yet to be named. How might we view the ministry of acolyting as a minor order, offering a way of discerning one's life in Christ in the everyday moments of school, play, work, and friendships?

FAITH DEVELOPMENT, YOUTH, AND WORSHIP

We begin to know God at an early age from those who nurture us, our environment, and the experiences we see, hear, touch, and taste. As Jeremiah has written, "Before I formed you in the womb, I knew you, and before you were born I consecrated you" (Jer. 1:5). A story has been shared by many of a toddler who sought to be alone with their newborn sibling, just home from the hospital. Parents listening in heard them ask the infant, "Tell me about God. I am beginning to forget."

Ana-Maria Rizzuto believes that children first become conscious of God between two and three years of age. Childhood images of God, she asserts, are powerful and influence us through a lifetime.[10] At the core of Rizzuto's understanding of how individuals grow in a relationship with the living God is the concept of *transitional object representation*. This includes those sensory experiences we have at worship. It is also the place where adults' imagination and creative processes work, where we "play around" with our perceptions of material, relational, and spiritual realities to discover meaning and where we envision new ways of responding to God in the future. Serving at God's altar can create such transitional spaces. In each stage of our faith formation, the image of God must grow and be redefined, using new capacities of reasoning and relating so that the current understanding of God is adequate for the challenges of the new stage of life, whether it be childhood, adolescence, young adulthood, or full maturity.

Children need direct experience with the physical world if they are to develop cognitively. Faith and belief in God can be considered abstract concepts, so most individuals—children under the age of twelve especially—need to gather data from concrete

---

9. In the Roman Catholic Church, becoming an instituted acolyte comes during the first year when one is in seminary, the first step in their formation for ordination to the priesthood. As instituted acolytes, they have the responsibility of assisting priests and deacons in carrying out their liturgical ministry. As special ministers of the Eucharist, these acolytes may also give Holy Communion to the faithful at the liturgy and to the sick and they can expose the Blessed Sacrament for adoration.

10. Ana-Maria Rizzuto, *The Birth of the Living God: A Psychoanalytic Study* (Chicago: University of Chicago Press, 1979), 7, 178.

experiences and test the validity of ideas through active experimentation. Discoveries made through direct experiences are more transformational and exciting for children than lessons in which adults tell them what they ought to know.

Faith communities are called to partner with parents in raising up our children in faith. One way the church can assist is to provide a structure of small groups that bring people together to support one another in their spiritual growth. It can be stimulated through a relationship with a mentor—an older person who becomes a spiritual friend to a younger person. Acolyte ministry provides for such an opportunity for children, youth, and adults.

In the Christian tradition, worship, at its heart, is an encounter with Christ. The words of St. Ambrose explain the encounter is available to us through scripture and the signs and symbols of our ritual's actions such as water and oil, bread and wine: "You have shown yourself to me, O Christ, face to face. I have met you in the sacraments."[11] As a community gathered in Christ's name, we repeat the ritual words and symbolic actions, allowing them to take root within us and, like a seed growing secretly, the fruit of the Spirit appears in its own time.

---

11. Frank T. Griswold, preface to *Enriching Our Worship* (New York: Church Publishing, 1998), 7.

CHAPTER TWO

Why We Serve

Therefore, since we are receiving a kingdom that cannot be shaken, let us give thanks, by which we offer to God an acceptable worship with reverence and awe. (Heb. 12:28)

WHERE DOES GOD MEET THE ACOLYTE on Sunday? This question could be posed to anyone at any time and in any location. But why do children and youth (and adults) answer the call to serve God at the altar during the worship on Sunday mornings (or other days and times) when there are plenty of other things to do tugging at their hearts, minds, and bodies? Attending church on Sunday mornings is no longer the only option available to families and individuals today. For young people, school activities and sports directly compete for their time and the lure of having one morning a week to sleep in has no age limits. Why do any of us show up on Sunday morning?

As humans made in the image of God, we yearn for the holy. We yearn to have the existential questions of life and death answered. We hunger to be part of a community that seeks wholeness. Sheryl Kujawa-Holbrook and Fredrica Harris Thompsett write:

> Wholeness, or holiness, is fundamental to the call of the baptized. Holiness, within a Christian context, goes beyond the notion of good behavior or even of being religious. Rather, it refers to our experience of God, deepened through life in the Christian community as it moves into the events of our daily lives.[12]

Parents and grandparents often bring their children to church for education, to be formed in a life of faith. And some of those young people watch the participants in the liturgy in action and wonder, "Can I do that?" When

---

12. Sheryl A. Kujawa-Holbrook and Fredrica Harris Thompsett, *Born of Water, Born of Spirit: Supporting the Ministry of the Baptized in Small Congregations* (Herndon, VA: The Alban Institute, 2010), 64.

asked why they serve, many acolytes of school age answer, "It's fun to help." "I like being up front and close to the action." "It feels special to be close to the altar." "It's not as boring as sitting in church." And then there is always, "I don't know; my mother signed me up." Whether they initially come of their own volition or by the insistence of a parent, those who stay and remain committed to this ministry do get something out of worship, otherwise they would never show up year after year. We believe, as James Fenhagan states, it is due to the "energy and vision we are given as a result of our encounter with the holiness of God."[13]

Fenhagen offers the following four functions as integral to all forms of Christian ministry. The ministry of the acolyte fulfills all of these by the various roles they play during worship. It would behoove us as mentors of acolytes to frame our approach in training to these purposes:

> *We are storytellers.* In ministry we must be able to articulate and own the story of our redemption and share it in ways others may hear.
>
> *We are value bearers.* We are sent into the world to bear witness to the gospel and the impact of its message on the whole of human experience.
>
> *We are community builders.* As the people of Pentecost we are called to be ambassadors of reconciliation throughout human societies.

> *We are spiritual journeyers.* We are people on a pilgrimage, always reaching for "holiness" and more authentic ways of living in the world.[14]

What if our goals in the training of acolytes for ministry focused on these aspects of ministry? What is learned and practiced as an acolyte: be prepared, pay attention, show humility, be respectful, and be ready for any possibility to happen are core attributes of a follower of Christ inside and outside the church.

TODAY'S RELIGIOUS SEEKER

Kit Carlson writes about the rising of the "Nones" in her research about the Millennial generation and their disappearance from the Church. This generation and the ones who come after them (who may still be attending church with their parents or are in our confirmation programs today) still seek encounters with the holy. Kit describes this cohort of "spiritually homeless" in three ways: the nomad, the prodigal, and the exile. She quotes Giles, a prodigal who did not connect his personal faith with his experience attending church:

> I liked actually *being* in church because I liked the idea of ritual. I enjoyed the beauty of the building, especially the stained glass, the organ, the music, the incense, when we had it. The pageantry of everything was really

---

13. James C. Fenhagen, *Mutual Ministry: New Vitality for the Local Church* (New York: Seabury, 1977), 26.
14. Ibid., 26–30.

enjoyable for me. I remember being excited to be an acolyte. I remember avoiding Sunday school on a regular basis. I would hide in the janitor's closet when I was supposed to be in Sunday school. I think eventually my parents figured that out.[15]

We wonder, what if his acolyte mentor had been more intentional about his participation in the liturgy? One of the questions Carlson poses in *Speaking Our Faith* could also be asked of the young people in our churches (and their friends). Can this be applied to acolytes, even at a young age (borrowing from the apostle Paul):

> What would it look like if we focused on empowering and equipping our post-Boomer members to evangelize their peers? . . . How *are* they to call on one in whom they have not believed? And how *are* they to believe in one of whom they have never heard? And how *are* they to hear without someone to proclaim him?[16]

For children in our congregations, these existential questions may not have yet formed. Certainly, they are simmering within our youth who often make up the bulk of acolyte ranks in our parishes. Inside and outside our churches, parents seek the best for their children, including their spiritual development—even if this might be articulated as being good, being kind, being nice to others. One of the purposes in

education and formation in the Episcopal tradition is to let our children know that God is always present. By providing opportunities for all to learn about God, to come closer to Jesus Christ, and to be aware of the Holy Spirit is part of the experience of being an acolyte and seeker, a person who is on a lifelong journey of faith.

Robert Coles, noted child psychiatrist and anthropologist, has spent much of his work exploring the spiritual life of children.[17] He came to see children as young seekers, asking the deep questions of life more often and more intensely than most adults realize. Older children and adolescents try to make sense out of their lives; they want to understand what is happening and why. In that process they often turn to God or a spiritual resource outside of themselves. He discovered that this occurs in all children, even those whose families are not religious.

MENTORING ACOLYTES

Mentoring acolytes is not just about teaching the facts, terminology, and choreography. It is about understanding the space in which we worship God and learn how to inhabit it so that others may also experience the holy. Borrowing from Parker Palmer,

> To study with a teacher who not only speaks but listens, who not only gives answers but

---

15. Kit Carlson, *Speaking Our Faith: Equipping the Next Generations to Tell the Old, Old Story* (New York: Church Publishing, 2018), 29.
16. Ibid., 42.
17. Robert Coles, *The Spiritual Life of Children* (Boston: Houghton Mifflin, 1990).

asks questions and welcomes our insights, who provides information and theories that do not close doors but open new ones, who encourages students to help each other learn—to study with a teacher is to know the power of learning space.[18]

Palmer speaks of a learning space as one that has openness, boundaries, and an air of hospitality. This could also be applied to worship and how we engage acolytes in coming to learn their part in the holy work that they perform.

As leaders, we must be open to the questions posed to us, and open to the encounters and experiences each of us may have while serving. Acolytes need to be open to the possibility of providing a bridge for another to encounter the Holy. For example, one morning in the sacristy as the altar party (priest, eucharistic ministers, and acolytes) gathered for prayer before worship, a prayer was offered by the presider. Upon its conclusion, an eleven-year-old, serving as a torchbearer for the first time, added his own prayer asking that our worship [today] remember those who are hurting in the world. The space was open. It was an unexpected, holy moment in which the rest of the altar party was left speechless.

Adults need to model the boundaries that we share when serving at God's altar. Worship has a structure, and in the Episcopal Church we follow a certain order to our liturgy. While offering silence that is permeable, acolytes are most helpful when they know the rhythm and flow of the service; transitions in liturgy are often times that acolytes perform their duties. Acolytes who are comfortable in knowing what is happening and why, as well as their role in the action, will add integrity to worship for others as well as themselves. Their anxiousness will cease and their confidence will grow along with their leadership with their acolyte partners. Lastly, just like worship, acolyte ministry is about hospitality. It is central to the biblical story of God welcoming the stranger and using the stranger to introduce us to the unexpected. It is through a welcoming, open environment that we can discern how God is calling us.

The ministry of an acolyte is a four-fold ministry of service to the Lord's altar. Being an acolyte provides an interactive and "up front" experience of leading worship. They develop a competency in the language and movements of the liturgy and grow in spiritual maturity as they fulfill the expectations of their duties while serving over a period of time, perhaps beginning in late childhood through adolescence. Serving God's people and modeling discipleship in worship is a skill that is transferrable to ministry outside the doors of our churches. Introducing young people to a way of life and creating their own "manifesto" (declaration of purpose) can become part of acolyte training (see the appendix for more) to support this lifelong journey.

---

18. Parker J. Palmer, *To Know As We Are Known: Education as a Spiritual Journey* (San Francisco: HarperSanFrancisco, 1993), 70–71.

DISCERNING A CALL TO ACOLYTE MINISTRY

Now there are varieties of gifts, but the same Spirit; and there are varieties of services, but the same Lord; and there are varieties of activities, but it is the same God who activates all of them in everyone. To each is given the manifestation of the Spirit for the common good. To one is given through the Spirit the utterance of wisdom, and to another the utterance of knowledge according to the same Spirit, to another faith by the same Spirit, to another gifts of healing by the one Spirit, to another the working of miracles, to another prophecy, to another the discernment of spirits, to another various kinds of tongues, to another the interpretation of tongues. All these are activated by one and the same Spirit, who allots to each one individually just as the Spirit chooses. (1 Cor. 12:4-11)

First Corinthians 12 tells us that each of us is given different gifts to serve the community and we are all a part of the body of Christ working together. An invitation to ministry, rather than recruitment, is a hospitable way to seek adults and young people to serve as acolytes. Perhaps you have perceived the gifts of listening, serving, and helping others in members of your congregation.

Episcopal Relief and Development has developed a series of exercises to help a congregation in its discernment of gifts for ministry. A variety of assessments are available to download for the gifts of the "head, heart, and human" attributes we all possess on their website.[19] Depending on your context and those who are seeking to find where their gifts meet the needs of liturgical ministry, these sources may be helpful to use with youth and adults.

While we do not tend to think of being an acolyte as a vocation, our invitation can be seen as a call to the individual to exercise their gifts in new ways. Following a call requires the need for training: the nuts and bolts of the roles to be played, the importance of the ministry, and how each individual has recognized gifts appropriate to it.

---

19. "Gifts Discernment Resources," Episcopal Relief and Development, accessed May 15, 2018, *http://calledtotransformation.org/gifts-discernment/gifts-discernment-resources/*.

CHAPTER THREE

How We Worship

Again Jesus spoke to them, saying, "I am the light of the world. Whoever follows me will never walk in darkness but will have the light of life." (John 8:12)

WORSHIP HAS BEEN PART of the human condition since the beginning of time. We have always reached to the beyond, to wonder and explore the mystery of the unknown, what we as Christians call God. This yearning for answers about who we are and whose we are is grounded in our need to be in relationship—with one another and our creator. The word *worship* comes from *weorthscripe*, similar to *worthship* in today's vernacular. In worship we praise God, respond to God in prayer, and remember the holy, life-giving acts of Jesus through the sacrament of Holy Baptism and Holy Eucharist. Worship is a dialogue, a conversation of give-and-take between a worshiper and God, whether done silently and alone or in community. In worshiping with others, our *leitourgia*—liturgy—truly becomes the work of the people. It is an active verb that helps us become refreshed Christians time after time, repeating again and again the traditions that have been passed down through the ages.

Acolytes are active participants in the liturgies of the Church. Perhaps one of the most recognized roles of an acolyte is that of lighting and extinguishing candles. The presence of the light reminds us of Jesus coming into our world and into our lives. An acolyte carrying a torch into the sanctuary in procession is a symbol of Jesus coming into the presence of the worshiping community. Just as it illuminated the Word of God in ancient times before the advent of electricity, today it enlightens the Gospel as it is read in our midst. And as acolytes carry the light out, they remind us that we are to carry the light of Christ into the world.

Churches of all denominations have an order to their worship that typically include an entrance, proclamation and response, thanksgiving and communion, and sending forth into the world with a blessing. The Service of the Word (lessons and preaching) comes to us from the Hebrew synagogue service. Thanksgiving, or Service of the Table (Holy Eucharist or Lord's Supper), reenacts the meal Jesus shared with his disciples in the Upper Room in Jerusalem before his arrest, crucifixion, and death. We see how the early order of worship came to be developed after the story of the walk to Emmaus:

> Now on that same day two of them were going to a village called Emmaus, about seven miles from Jerusalem, and talking with each other about all these things that had happened. While they were talking and discussing, Jesus himself came near and went with them, but their eyes were kept from recognizing him. . . . Then beginning with Moses and all the prophets, he interpreted to them the things about himself in all the scriptures. As they came near the village to which they were going, he walked ahead as if he were going on. But they urged him strongly, saying, "Stay with us, because it is almost evening and the day is now nearly over." So he went in to stay with them. When he was at the table with them, he took bread, blessed and broke it, and gave it to them. Then their eyes were opened, and they recognized him; and he vanished from their sight. (Luke 24:13–16, 27–31)

Sharing stories and praise, opening up the scripture, praying for ourselves and others, and responding with a meal together are at the heart of our worship life as a Christian community.

HOW DO WE TEACH ABOUT WORSHIP?

> Jesus said, ". . . Believe me, the hour is coming when you will worship the Father neither on this mountain nor in Jerusalem. You worship what you do not know; we worship what we know, for salvation is from the Jews. But the hour is coming, and is now here, when the true worshipers will worship the Father in spirit and truth, for the Father seeks such as these to worship him." (John 4:21-23)

How many of us truly worship what we know? We may have been taught about the Triune God, but have we experienced being in the presence of the Lord? There is a diversity of worship styles and traditions in the Episcopal Church, but in every one of them, God is present as Creator, Redeemer, and Sustainer (Father, Son, and Holy Spirit). Whether it is a Rite I or Rite II Eucharist, Morning Prayer, or Evensong, how an individual congregation worships is a witness to their experience of the Holy One.

As church leaders, we must rely on young people learning about worship from their experiences of being in church. Some congregations try to address this need with a lecture, either in confirmation preparation or another classroom environment. However, to really form an understanding of worship, to actually "know" it, we must speak about it, show it, and include young people in it as leaders, not observers. The old proverb says: "Tell me, and I'll forget. Show me and I may remember. Involve me and I'll understand." This statement is a formation process. As a person educating others about worship, intentionally following this process will lead to the most complete understanding:

- Clearly define the goals you hope to achieve in the preparation process.
- Collect and master a body of knowledge that is relevant to your contextual worship expression.
- Design an experience that tells, shows, and includes.

In our experience, the following goals seem to best meet the needs of congregations, young people, parents, and leaders. Participants will:

- Understand why we worship.
- Incorporate the design and execution of Episcopal worship as a guide that influences their faith development.
- Be able to fully participate in their worshiping community.
- Be offered the best possible environment to experience God.

Your goals may be different, but these four identified goals come from the varied experiences we have gained from traveling around the breadth of worship within the Episcopal Church. Wrestle with your acolytes and research your own goals and the body of knowledge that drives them. The body of knowledge most relevant to these goals is summed up below.

Why We Worship

Worship itself is an expression of our adoration and respect for God. In Romans, Paul says:

> I appeal to you therefore, brothers and sisters, by the mercies of God, to present your bodies as a living sacrifice, holy and acceptable to God, which is your spiritual worship. Do not be conformed to this world, but be transformed by the renewing of your minds, so that you may discern what is the will of God—what is good and acceptable and perfect. (Rom. 12:1–2)

We *present our bodies* by giving up our time and putting ourselves entirely into an act of worship *as a living sacrifice*. We hope that all people who serve the altar know that the time they give is important and valuable. If they don't, we need to tell them. The time spent at church, the words we speak, the songs we sing, the movements we make, and the emotions we feel are all *living sacrifices* of the body made to God in worship. Our existence alone is pleasing to God—we do not need anything else to prove our worth of the grace God gives us. But how do we understand the word *existence*? One who comes to church for an hour or so to disengage and check off a box is not fully alive. When our bodies are here but without the intention of this living sacrifice, we are not engaged in true and proper worship. This is obvious when we look at preteens and teenagers. They will show you, quite obviously, whether they have the tools and interest to be engaged or not.

Do not conform to this world, but be transformed by the renewing of your minds. It is easy in a world of YouTube channels and memes to be constantly searching for the next funny, sexy, or dramatic experience with which to engage. The pattern of this twenty-first-century world changes every ten to thirty seconds. Our minds are tired; we are bombarded by so many moments of sensory overload, information, and decision-making that most times we are not fully present to anything—we just pull out a phone and zone out (which is a different action than "disengaging"). In worship, we change gears from the normal, which gives us time to renew our minds. Worship gives us moments of clarity and peace, which always carries a message (whether we hear it or not). That message inspires a reaction within us that, when tested, proves to be either from God or not. Those messages that are *good, acceptable, and perfect,* or at least feel that way to us when we are fully engaged in worship, can be trusted as God's will, delivered to us by the mechanism of worship, following the design of liturgy.

As altar servers, our worship experience is different from that of a person sitting in a pew. As acolytes, we are not only participants in worship, but also servant leaders of it on behalf of the congregation. We assist the other ministers in the presentation of the story of our redemption, and in doing so we are afforded an opportunity that is not available to all. As the celebrant breaks the consecrated bread and pours wine into the chalice, we are recalling and remembering the story of Jesus' sacrifice for the sins of the world. We are swept up into the story of Christ's redemption, and the gift of imagination serves the sacramental work of using the natural as the means to experience the supernatural. To come to this experience and only partially engage it, or disengage from it entirely, leads to a missed opportunity and disappointment. How do we prepare for this momentous event every week? We gain understanding of the intricacies of how the liturgy is designed to tell us a story, and we engage that story with all of our senses.

Worship as a Guide That Influences Our Faith Development

Worship is guided by religious rites. A rite is a ceremony or ritual that is used to direct our adoration and respect for God. Holy Baptism, the Celebration and Blessing of a Marriage, Holy Eucharist, Ordination of a Deacon, Confirmation, Burial of the Dead, and the Daily Office are a few examples of rites contained in the Book of Common Prayer. These rites are formal, dignified, and holy. Everything that defines who we are as Christians and specifically as Episcopalians is found in our liturgies.

Liturgies follow a progression. They move us through a process that has evolved over thousands of years. The design and process of Episcopal worship is simple:

1. *We gather.* By means of prayer and song, we focus our attention.

2. *We hear the Word of God.* We are attentive to God's message that is delivered through Holy Scripture. We are assisted by trained orators (lectors) and preachers to give us context, inspiration, and conviction based on the Word.

3. *We respond to the Word of God.* We proclaim our faith statement. We pray for the world and ourselves. We confess our sins.

4. *We make peace.* We pass along the joy of reconciliation and receive it back from our neighbors.

5. *We offer our thanks.* We realign our attitudes to one of gratitude.

6. *We re–member the story.* This is both a retelling and reuniting ourselves with Jesus and with each other.

7. *We receive the sacrament.* We take into ourselves the outward and physical signs of the inward spiritual grace that is the quintessence of our worship, literally taking God into ourselves in order to carry God out into the world.

8. *We are sent.* We depart from the worshiping community to do the work God has given us to do.

This process is a formative one; it isn't about what happens on Sunday mornings, but about what happens in our lives. No matter where we are in our cognitive (or faith) development, we learn by practice and experience. Let's translate this pattern into how we grow in faith and mature in our relationship with God and one another by comparing it to how we learn in a classroom. It might look something like this:

1. We gather. What's the beginning ritual of the class? Attendance? Review? It's the same at every session.

2. We hear the lesson of the day.

3. We ask and answer questions about the lesson of the day.

4. We practice the lesson with each other.

5. We find ways that the lesson affects us in real life.

6. We tell our story by means of the lesson, testing our understanding and comprehension of it.

7. We are affirmed in our understanding of the lesson.

8. We are sent to live our lives with the lesson in our minds.

Our worship is the literal process by which we are formed. The above process is the roadmap that outlines a process of education—how we learn and incorporate those learnings into our life. You could teach history, theory, or practice using this model. It is the same with

Christian formation. When acolytes make this connection, they can more fully engage worship because they are now actively looking at it for the life-changing moments. Without this understanding, worship is just something you do because you are supposed to. Our best hope becomes learning by osmosis, praying that something works its way into the brain over time.

Fully Participating in the Worship Community

In the Episcopal Church, we are all full members of the community by virtue of our baptism. All are invited and encouraged to participate in and receive the sacrament of the Holy Eucharist. For some congregations, this means that children are often with their peers in Sunday school during the liturgy of the Word, hearing the stories of God at age-appropriate levels. They join their families and other adults for The Great Thanksgiving at the time of the offertory in the sanctuary. For other congregations, all ages (depending on ability and training) are able to serve as ushers, readers or lectors, and oblationers. As noted previously, we are formed in faith by the experiences we share with one another. Stuart Childs writes as a sixth grader his experience of worship:

My parents have taken me to Sunday school for a long time. Over time, God and Church have become very special to me. Everybody has their own relationship with God. Now I know

I am only eleven, but I still feel like I have a pretty good relationship with him. I would like to make it better (most people would). We get so caught up in our daily lives (me in particular) that we don't "get around to it."

When I'm in church, I try to take it as a time to improve my relationship with God. In church, I have a window of opportunity to pray and get a feeling of peace before the wave picks me back up and puts me right out into the world again.

Although it takes awhile for me to realize it, I love being in the church and the feeling of peace and love that fills me while I'm there. These are the times when I feel all week long and "do the things that you would have us to do" then I can really be happy.[20]

In order for children to understand who we are as Episcopalians, they must be present to experience the flow of our liturgy. From entrance procession to hearing the stories of God's people, from bringing our alms and oblations to the altar, and from hearing Jesus's words of consecration, taking Jesus into our bodies, and being dismissed with a blessing, our words and actions affirm and acknowledge our belonging to the family of God.

Creating an Environment to Experience God

"The Episcopal Church Welcomes You" is seen on countless street corners and signs near our

---

20. Stuart Childs, "A Child's Faith," in *Liturgy as Formation* (New York: Domestic and Foreign Missionary Society, 2003), 58.

church sidewalks. How do we create an environment where all are truly welcome? In today's world in which our liturgy may be unfamiliar, one way is having a worship bulletin that helps one follow along and participate in the liturgy. Balancing a Book of Common Prayer along with several hymnals can be a barrier. In addition, having worship leaders who "lead" by word and example is important. This is often an unstated role of an acolyte.

Understanding the structure and flow of the liturgy is helpful, but not everyone in the congregation is steeped in "why we do what we do." Ralph Blackman, former dean of St. James Cathedral in Chicago, shared at the 2003 conference "Will Our Children Have Faith? Christian Formation from Generation to Generation" his perceptions:

> Think of the structure of worship, the words and music and space we use. Reflect upon how the liturgy includes or excludes. A model I have found helpful is to think of the Eucharist as an extended family feast—which in my personal situation literally includes a broad cross-section of race, ethnicity, wealth, age, etc. At such gatherings there is room for the old to reminisce—tell their stories, and the young to dream—tell their stories, and for those in the middle years to, well, tell their stories. And there is room for all to play and eat, to engage the fullness of family and life as is appropriate and as they are able. The family drama is enriched by each new addition no matter how they enter the extending circle. It isn't perfect. It certainly isn't always neat and tidy. It never fits into the time subscribed. And it is always full of surprises, interruptions, and last minute adjustments. But it is real and honest.[21]

Yes, worship can be messy—but the play and drama of liturgy helps us to encounter the Incarnate God. Those who serve at God's altar assist in providing the atmosphere while literally setting the table in which all are welcome to experience the Living God.

---

21. Ralph Blackman, "Invitation and Hospitality in Worship," in *Liturgy as Formation* (New York: Domestic and Foreign Missionary Society, 2003), 5–6.

CHAPTER FOUR

An Instructed Eucharist in Word and Image

Jesus said to her, "Woman, believe me, the hour is coming when you will worship the Father neither on this mountain nor in Jerusalem. You worship what you do not know; we worship what we know, for salvation is from the Jews. But the hour is coming, and is now here, when the true worshipers will worship the Father in spirit and truth, for the Father seeks such as these to worship him." (John 4:21–23)

IN COLLEGE, ROGER'S ART PROFESSORS routinely stated, "You must master the rules and be a master of following them, so that someday you may masterfully break them." When his altar servers and acolytes proclaim that worship is boring, his typical reply is, "Then you don't know what we're doing or why we do it." How many of us truly worship what we know? We have been taught about the Triune God—Father, Son, and Holy Spirit—but have we experienced being in the presence of the Lord? After twenty years (for Roger) and thirty-five years (for Sharon) of ministry in the church and a lifetime of using the Book of Common Prayer, we're pretty sure we still haven't witnessed the entire spectrum of worship styles and traditions in our church. However, in every one of the hundreds of cultural expressions of the Holy Eucharist Rite I or II we have witnessed, we have found God in spirit while witnessing a congregation's truth.

An instructed Holy Communion is a useful tool for explaining what we do in worship and why we do it, but the typical format (that is, students stand in a ring around the altar while a priest talks) only appeals to one learning style. What follows is an integrated method of instructed Eucharist, including visuals, spoken words, and experience. You will find illustrations to create your own guided Eucharist that closely follows your congregation's service for use in your acolyte training in the appendix.

THE LITURGY OF THE WORD

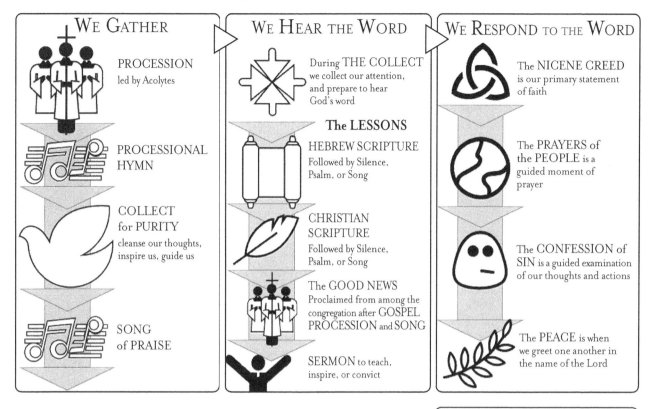

WE GATHER

PROCESSION
led by Acolytes

PROCESSIONAL HYMN

COLLECT for PURITY
cleanse our thoughts, inspire us, guide us

SONG of PRAISE

WE HEAR THE WORD

During THE COLLECT we collect our attention, and prepare to hear God's word

The LESSONS

HEBREW SCRIPTURE
Followed by Silence, Psalm, or Song

CHRISTIAN SCRIPTURE
Followed by Silence, Psalm, or Song

The GOOD NEWS
Proclaimed from among the congregation after GOSPEL PROCESSION and SONG

SERMON to teach, inspire, or convict

WE RESPOND TO THE WORD

The NICENE CREED is our primary statement of faith

The PRAYERS of the PEOPLE is a guided moment of prayer

The CONFESSION of SIN is a guided examination of our thoughts and actions

The PEACE is when we greet one another in the name of the Lord

The procession is the first movement of the service and it *begins in song*. Since the fourth century, Christians have begun the Holy Eucharist with an entrance rite in which the presider and other ministers of the liturgy move to their places in the assembly. The entrance rite prepares us to hear the Word of God as we acknowledge by our praise and acclamation our gratitude to the God whose grace makes our very gathering possible.

The acolytes first appear as a leader of worship leading the way, followed by choir and other liturgical leaders—lay and ordained. While the congregation sings, the worship space is filled with music, and the worship leaders process to the altar with worship instruments: crosses, torches or candles, incense, and even banners.

The opening acclamation is a loud and enthusiastic opening to the service. It changes depending on the church season and the celebrant's discretion. During the season of Easter, it is where we hear the first "Alleluia! Christ is Risen!" with the response, "The Lord is risen indeed! Alleluia!"

WE GATHER

PROCESSION
led by Acolytes

PROCESSIONAL HYMN

COLLECT for PURITY
cleanse our thoughts, inspire us, guide us

SONG of PRAISE

The collect for purity is offered. The word *collect* comes from Latin and means "to gather." The collect for purity is a gathering prayer wherein we acknowledge God's power and authority, we ask God to cleanse our hearts, inspire us, and make us ready to be fully present during this time. If you zone out here, then you've missed the prayer designed to bring you in and fully engage you.

A song of praise follows. We sing at worship as a congregation because it unites us, teaches us about God, and recalls a most ancient tradition of humans singing together.

WE HEAR THE WORD

During THE COLLECT we collect our attention, and prepare to hear God's word

The LESSONS

HEBREW SCRIPTURE
Followed by Silence, Psalm, or Song

CHRISTIAN SCRIPTURE
Followed by Silence, Psalm, or Song

The GOOD NEWS
Proclaimed from among the congregation after GOSPEL PROCESSION and SONG

SERMON to teach, inspire, or convict

The collect of the day brings the entrance rite to its conclusion and anticipates the scripture readings of the liturgy. It changes every Sunday and reflects an aspect of religious life inspired by the readings, festival days, or themes described in the Revised Common Lectionary.

The lessons are the means by which God speaks to us. They change week to week and follow a three-year cycle of readings called the lectionary. The lessons begin with one to two readings: one from Hebrew Scripture found in the Old Testament, and one from the Christian Scriptures found in the New Testament. The readings are typically read by a member of the congregation. The natural home for Holy Scripture is the liturgy of the Church, as God's people hear the Word of God in human words, just as they continue to offer human words and actions in the worship of God. Each reading is followed by silence, the psalm appointed to correspond to the readings, or a song. The third lesson is from one of the four Gospels, telling the Good News of Jesus Christ; it is read by a deacon or priest, called the Gospeller. A **gospel procession**, usually accompanied by song and led by the processional cross and torches (carried by acolytes), someone holding the Gospel Book, and sometimes a thurifer. The Gospel is read among the people to proclaim the gospel appointed of the day.

The sermon is presented by the preacher, who may or may not be the celebrant (leader) of the rite. A sermon is a formal speech prepared by a learned individual and guides the congregation in their response to the Holy Scripture.

It is the hinge point between the proclamation of the Word and our response; it can teach, inspire, and/or send the congregation forward in action to live out the Word in daily life.

Our response to the proclamation of the Word comes when the entire assembly reaffirms their faith and offers communal prayers. In early Christian liturgies, the "creed" of the church—the content of the church's faith—was the sweeping summary of salvation history in the eucharistic prayer.

The Nicene Creed, developed in the fourth century as a contrast to beliefs we have come to define as heresy, began to appear as a summary of faith in the liturgies of the sixth-century Western Church. It is spoken in unison while standing. We do this to declare our singular belief in its words and to display our solidarity with each other and with God. The Nicene Creed is our primary statement of faith and what we believe in.

The Prayers of the People is a guided method of prayer and the moment where we are most active in being in the Spirit. In the intercessions, the priestly people of God (all of us) show themselves to be the very Body of Christ by continuing his high priestly ministry, lifting up the needs and concerns of the world to God. During these prayers and responses, we pray for:

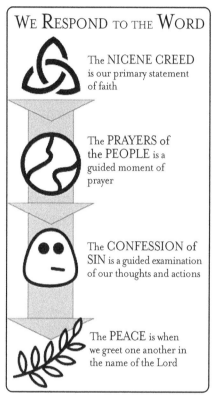

WE RESPOND TO THE WORD

The NICENE CREED is our primary statement of faith

The PRAYERS of the PEOPLE is a guided moment of prayer

The CONFESSION of SIN is a guided examination of our thoughts and actions

The PEACE is when we greet one another in the name of the Lord

- The Universal Church, its members, and its mission
- The nation and all in authority
- The welfare of the world
- The concerns of the local community
- Those who suffer and those in any trouble
- The departed, and the saints of the church if appropriate

In the Prayers of the People, we actively and humbly call upon God's will to heal, guide, strengthen, and bless God's creation.

The confession of sin is led by the deacon or celebrant and is a structured guide to recognizing that we have sinned in our thoughts, words, and deeds. We confess the memories we know, and we confess those things we are not aware of as well. We confess the sinful actions we have taken, and the action God called us to that we did not follow through with. We acknowledge that we have not loved God with our complete person. We confess that we have not loved our neighbors as ourselves. We then ask, out of consideration for Jesus, that God has mercy on us and forgives us. We commit to following God's good, pleasing, and perfect will, so that we live according to Jesus's teaching, and bring glory to God.

The Peace is where ministers and people greet one another in the name of the Lord. We bring the Lord into our relationships through peace. "May the Peace of the Lord be always with you." You can feel the mood of the room lighten and the peace of God actually descends on the people during this portion of the liturgy. This is the time to prepare yourself for Holy Communion. Is there someone you need to make peace with before meeting the risen Christ at the altar of God? After we share the peace that is ours by God's grace, we present ourselves to God in the symbols of bread and wine that God has given and human hands have made. We offer these to God as we move to the second "movement" of our liturgy:

THE HOLY COMMUNION

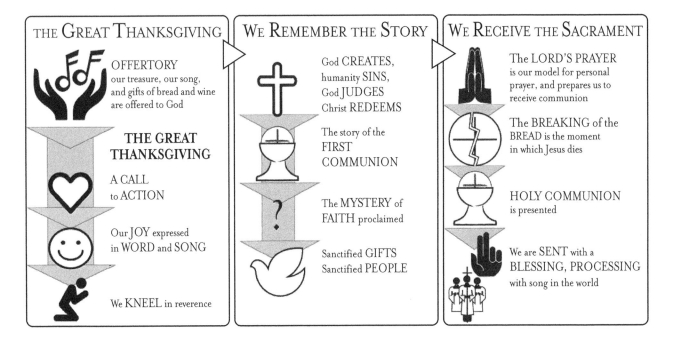

The movements of the Holy Communion follow the narrative of God's redemption of creation.

The offertory begins this portion of the rite. We offer our talent in song. We offer our time in contemplation. We offer our treasure in financial or spiritual gifts. We present these gifts alongside gifts of bread and wine. During this time, a deacon (if present) or a eucharistic minister or acolyte assists the celebrant in setting the altar and preparing it for the sacramental meal to come. The acceptance of monetary offerings collected in alms basins from ushers are also presented at this time.

The Great Thanksgiving begins with the Sursum Corda in which we stand and lift up our hearts, giving thanks and praise to God in words or song. The celebrant continues the prayer on the congregation's behalf; the prayer shifts focus, and we kneel or stand as a sign of reverence as the story of God's redemption of humanity is told: how God created the world, how we broke it, and how God sent Christ to bring us back to God. In the context of that remembrance, we offer ourselves and our gifts for the Spirit to make Christ present *to* us in the gifts and present *in* us through our mission in his name.

We hear the story of the meal of bread and wine that Jesus shared with his disciples, offering them gifts of his body and blood, welcoming us into the New Covenant and asking us to remember him. We join together in proclaiming the mystery of our faith. We ask God, through the Holy Spirit, to change bread and wine into holy food and drink while changing us into holy saints to receive it. (This is called the *epiclesis* = calling down from on high.)

This is all part of the eucharistic prayer—an act of thanksgiving for God's mighty acts, especially for the saving work wrought by Christ, with an invocation to the Holy Spirit to transform the bread and wine and, through them, unite the assembly with Christ in his life and mission. At the end of the prayer the entire assembly says, "Amen": an assent to the presider's words and a commitment to receive what God has been asked to give. It should be noted that this prayer is not a reenactment of the Lord's Supper; it is a current enactment of what Jesus asked his disciples to do in memory of him.[22]

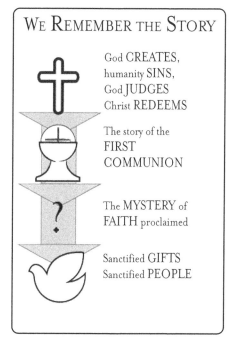

---

22. Patrick Malloy, *Celebrating The Eucharist: A Practical Ceremonial Guide for Clergy and Other Liturgical Ministers* (New York: Church Publishing, 2007), 130.

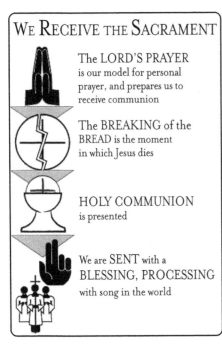

We Receive the Sacrament

The LORD'S PRAYER is our model for personal prayer, and prepares us to receive communion

The BREAKING of the BREAD is the moment in which Jesus dies

HOLY COMMUNION is presented

We are SENT with a BLESSING, PROCESSING with song in the world

The Lord's Prayer teaches us to pray and prepares us to witness the sacrifice of Jesus as we boldly declare God as "our father." The church fathers saw in the expression "daily bread" a reference to the Eucharist as well as to other foods. In its position between the eucharistic prayer and the breaking of the bread, the Lord's Prayer functions both as a climactic extension of the great thanksgiving and as a prayer of preparation for communion.[23]

The breaking of the bread is the ceremonial moment in which Jesus offers himself as sacrifice for the whole world. Some of us mark this with song. It is the most ancient name for the Eucharist and its importance is palpable when all is silent as the presider physically breaks the bread for all to see. An anthem (*Fraction*) or song often follows this gesture.

The Holy Communion is sharing the gifts of God to the people of God. It is offered to every baptized Christian in attendance. Music is often played, with quiet anthems or hymns offered as the clergy and lay eucharistic ministers serve the communicants. We share the Body and Blood of Christ and so become the Body of Christ in our ministry to the world. As St. Augustine once said in speaking of the bread and wine of the Eucharist, "Be what you can see, and receive what you are."

The sending is when we offer thanks and praise to God for revealing a good, pleasing, and perfect will to us. We ask for God to send us into the world to love and serve as faithful witnesses of Christ our Lord. The celebrant then offers a blessing over the people, and the rite is concluded with the final movement in song as we are led by the worship team out of worship and into the ministry of our day-to-day lives.

CONCLUSION

Like all life-changing experiences, worship tells a story. It is a grand story of how God seeks each of us out and directs us to a fulfilling and meaningful life. Like all good stories, worship has movement that brings us into the drama, through it, and back home again. These movements each tell us a story of where we come from, who we are, and where we are going.

---

23. Howard E. Galley, *The Ceremonies of the Eucharist: A Guide to Celebration* (Cambridge, MA: Cowley Publications, 1989), 117.

Putting this all together presents the best possible environment and encouragement to individuals who seek a relationship with God in worship. To teach it, we have to combine verbal, visual, and kinetic experiences. In the appendix, we've included the walkthrough above in a guided Eucharist, along with an infographic of the components and a worksheet version of it. Schedule time during a training retreat or hold a guided Eucharist annually for your acolytes. Find time to create a space that is holy, quiet, and set aside just for those who serve at the altar in particular. Ask clergy to lead the worship, explaining each part as you walk through it, and ask each acolyte to complete the worksheet at each phase. Hearing the expert, seeing the process on paper, and experiencing it step-by-step at a slower pace than usual with their peers at a special time is a fantastic and well-rounded approach to giving acolytes a complete understanding of liturgy. They'll know, and can pass on, "What we do and why we do it."

CHAPTER FIVE

Artifacts and Memorials

KNOWING THE "TOOLS OF THE TRADE" by name and purpose is important to include in training. Some terms will not directly apply to their ministry, but these descriptions will be of assistance to you as a liturgical leader and mentor in understanding the multitude of *artifacts* (holy objects that are used in worship or as daily reminders to us of our beliefs, traditions, and identity as Christians) and *memorials* (sacred places where prayer or other actions related to remembering and reenacting our faith occurs). Everything that is within the sanctuary (worship space) of a church has a specific purpose and significance. Some may seem very ancient and impractical for today, but they have deep historical meanings that go back centuries which assist us in acknowledging the traditions that have been with the Christian Church since its foundation.

Depending on the history, piety, and other sacramental practices, each church has its own customs and traditions. Some have described these differences within the Episcopal Church as Anglo-Catholic (high church with smells and bells), low church (informal, yet respectful), or broad church (somewhere in between). One of the joys of being an Episcopalian is the choice we have to worship in a congregation that fits our own spiritual practice, belief, and piety while all still retain the same rite based on the Book of Common Prayer, only enacted ceremonially in slightly different ways. You may discover new terms and objects that don't exist in your parish. We have simply attempted to be as inclusive as possible in describing all the practices we have seen and experienced in our travels worshiping in congregations across the wide Episcopal Church.

What follows is a description of the various vestments, vessels (and other objects), paraments, and furniture that are used by clergy and laity in worship. While many of these may come under the care of altar guilds or are symbols of an order of the clergy, it is helpful to understand their history, purpose, and use. Again, knowing why something exists helps in learning why we do what we do as acolytes (or any other liturgical leader) in serving at God's altar. Scattered throughout you will notice illustrations that show them in context. A visual dictionary of specific items that are "handled" by acolytes that you can use in putting together your own customary for your acolytes and eucharistic ministers is found in the appendix.

VESTMENTS

The vestments (robes and other garments) worn at the Eucharist originate from the late Roman Empire, which was the dominant culture of the early Church. Vestments add formality, seriousness, and festivity to our rites. They show us that something special is happening that is not the ordinary of our everyday life out in the world. According to Patrick Malloy, "The Book of Common Prayer mentions only five vestments: the alb, surplice, rochet, stole, and tippet. It also refers to other vestments distinctive of the orders of the diaconate, presbyterate, and episcopate, but does not name them."[24] According to a survey conducted and reported to the 2004 General Convention of the Episcopal Church, the majority of congregations shared that the celebrant wears full eucharistic vestments (alb, stole, and chasuble) when presiding at the Eucharist.[26] Our vestments help create the holy space for worship; they are not costumes for a performance, but garments intended to focus the worshiping community on its purpose of being gathered to praise God.

A Dictionary of Vestments[26]

alb A white (Latin *albus*: white) linen tunic that extends to the ankles, worn with a rope cincture at the waist; intended to cover street clothes, this is the universal garment for all liturgical ministers (white, recalling the white baptismal dress worn by neophytes in the early Church).

amice A white oblong piece of cloth, "the helmet of Salvation," worn under other vestments to protect from perspiration and cover clothing.

A celebrant wearing a chausable over an alb and stole.

---

24. Patrick Malloy, *Celebrating the Eucharist: A Practical Ceremonial Guide for Clergy and Other Liturgical Ministers* (New York: Church Publishing, 2007), 47.

25. Ibid., 48.

26. For specific descriptions of these vestments and their history, we commend Patrick Malloy's *Celebrating the Eucharist*, pages 48–57.

biretta A square cap with three flat projections worn by clergy

cassock A close-fitting (typically black) plain, lightweight garment that extends to the ankles. It can have buttons down the center, or a double breast arrangement and is worn under other vestments. This was once the streetwear for clergy, and some continue this practice today. Bishops wear purple cassocks.

A priest giving a blessing while wearing a biretta.

cassock-alb A combination of the amice and alb worn in place of a cassock and surplice or amice, alb, and cincture.

chasuble The outermost liturgical vestment worn by the celebrant (priest or bishop) during the Holy Eucharist. Circular in shape with a hole to place it over the head, it is usually the appropriate color for the church season.

chimere This vestment is a loose black or scarlet robe without sleeves worn by a bishop over the rochet, adapted from a riding cloak.

cincture A thick rope or belt tied at the waist to secure an alb or cassock; sometimes called a girdle.

clericals Clothing that clergy wear on the street to identify their calling:

collar A clerical that closes at the back of the neck, worn by ordained persons.

neck band A style of clerical in which the clergy collar is fully exposed and surrounds the neck.

shirts or blouses Deacons and priests typically wear black clergy shirts, bishops wear purple.

tab-collar A style of clerical in which a tab represents the full collar denoting an ordained person.

cope An intricate, ornate cape worn by a bishop or celebrant in festal processions fastened at the neck; historically worn to keep warm.

A bishop administering communion wearing a rochet, chimere, and stole.

cotta A surplice, but shorter and with shorter sleeves, sometimes no sleeves at all, and typically worn by acolytes or choristers.

dalmatic A knee-length, wide-sleeved tunic often worn by deacons.

maniple A ceremonial handkerchief that is worn on the left forearm.

mitre Headwear worn by a bishop, symbolizing their office.

A cathedral dean wears a cope over her vestments.

scapular A sleeveless tunic worn over an alb, typically by acolytes.

skull cap/zucchetto A beanie-type head garment worn by clergy, black for deacons and priests, purple for bishops.

Mitre

stole A long, narrow, often decorated piece of fabric draped around the neck to signify an ordained person. Priests and bishops wear the stole over both shoulders so that the two ends fall down over the chest to the legs; deacons wear it over only the left shoulder.

surplice A very full knee- to ankle-length lightweight white garment worn over a cassock that is gathered at the neck and with wide sleeves.

tippet A scarf worn by clergy and lay ministers around the neck that reaches midthigh. Ordained people wear black tippets, lay leaders wear blue.

tunic (tunicle) A shorter vestment worn over an alb by a deacon.

Two deacons, one as the Gospeller in procession holding the Gospel Book with a stole and alb, the other wearing a dalmatic.

SACRED VESSELS AND OBJECTS

There are a number of vessels used in worship in the Episcopal Church, especially during the Holy Eucharist. Those that are considered "sacred" are ones that come in contact with the consecrated elements (bread and wine) of the Eucharist. All of these items are often handled by acolytes and should be treated with respect.

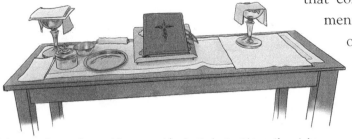

A free-standing credence table prepared for the Eucharist. Objects (from left to right): lavabo towel; chalice covered with a purificator, pall, and corporal; round bread box with a lid; lavabo bowl; extra paten; Missal on a missal stand; and extra chalice with a purificator.

Advent wreath A circle of greens with four (or five) candles to mark the passage of the four Sundays in Advent (plus Christmas with the fifth "Christ Candle"), lit consecutively week by week. It either hangs or is put on a stand in the chancel.

alms basin (*or offertory plate*) The large metal plate (bowl, basket, or other container) used to gather and present the money offerings of the congregation.

aspergillum A branch, brush, or perforated metal globe used to sprinkle holy water over the congregation.

banner A long piece of cloth depicting symbols, logos, or other designs that is either hung in the sanctuary or carried on a pole in procession.

baptismal shell A shallow vessel, often in the shape of a scallop shell, used at baptism to pick up water from the font and pour it upon the head of the one being baptized.

Bible Meaning library, a collection of sixty-six books describing the story of God's people and God's work of redemption through Jesus Christ.

bier A movable stand on which a casket rests during the Rite of Burial of the Dead.

boat A small decorative container, with a lid and spoon, that holds unburnt incense before it is placed in the thurible.

bread box A small ornamental box made of wood, stone, or metal that is used to bring unconsecrated bread or wafers (hosts) to the altar at the offertory.

candle lighter/extinguisher A long pole with a two-pronged end. One side is a tube into which is placed a taper (or container of oil) with a wick and a knob to raise and lower the

An oblations table with alms basins (one on top of the other), a flagon, and a bread box at the beginning of the liturgy.

taper; the other is a bell-shaped snuffer to extinguish the candles. Sometimes called a taper.

candles

> *eucharistic candles* Set on or near the altar during services that include Holy Communion.
>
> *office lights* Pairs of multiple candles on one base used in services of the Daily Office, such as Morning Prayer or Evening Prayer.
>
> *pascal candle* (see page 35)
>
> *sanctuary lamp* (eternal flame, chancel lamp, everlasting light) Represents the presence of Christ, and remains lit at all times, usually in a glass container near the reserved sacrament. (see page 35)
>
> *torch* A combustible light source used in processions. Originally carried to just give light in darkened buildings, it has come to represent bringing the fire of the Holy Spirit and the Light of Christ into a religious rite.

chalice A metal or ceramic cup with a footed base into which wine (and a little water) for the Eucharist is poured.

charcoal Self-igniting tablets of combustible material used for burning incense.

chrism Blessed oil, usually composed of pure olive oil and either balsam or another sweet perfume. There are oils of blessing, and oils of healing. Each are used differently and are typically consecrated by a bishop on Holy Tuesday when clergy annually renew their ordination vows.

ciborium A covered metal or ceramic vessel shaped as a chalice and used for holding consecrated hosts reserved in a tabernacle or aumbry.

cochlear (spoon) A perforated or slotted spoon used to remove any foreign materials from the chalice of consecrated wine during Holy Communion.

collection plate See *alms basin*.

cross

> *altar* A central cross resting on or affixed above the altar, used as a focal point during Holy Communion
>
> *pectoral* A cross worn by a liturgical leader on their chest suspended from their neck by a chain or cord.
>
> *processional* A staff with an ornamental cross at its top. In the absence of a verger or thurifer, the processional cross leads processions.

crozier The bishop's staff representing a shepherd's crook made of metal or wood.

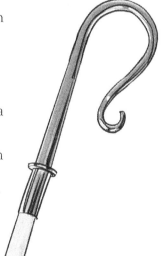

A bishop's crozier

crucifix A statue, carving, or other artwork depicting the crucified Jesus.

cruet A small container of glass or crystal for wine and water to be used at the Eucharist.

diptych A piece of artwork, usually decorating an altar, composed of two wooden panels hinged at the center.

elements The bread and wine to be consecrated at the Eucharist.

ewer A large, sometimes ornamental jug, used for carrying larger quantities of wine used during Holy Communion or water for Holy Baptism.

flagon A large, sometimes ornamental pitcher of precious metal with a hinged lid, used for carrying larger quantities of wine used during Holy Communion.

funeral pall A cloth that covers a casket or urn at a funeral.

Gospel Book A decorative book containing only the Gospel readings from the lectionary. It is typically processed to be among the congregation and read from by the Gospeller (a priest or deacon).

Holy Water Consecrated (blessed) water.

host Communion wafers, communion bread, large wafer, or other names that describe the bread used during Holy Communion to represent the Body of Christ. The host is typically the bread or large wafer that the priest "breaks" at the Fraction during the eucharistic prayer.

incense Material consisting of biological material (bark, oil, plant matter, etc.) that produces a fragrant smoke when burned. Represents a congregation's prayers ascending to heaven.

lavabo bowl *Lavabo* means "I shall wash." It is a small bowl, typically metal or glass, used to wash hands after the preparation of Holy Communion.

Missal *(service or altar book)* A book containing all liturgical rites necessary for celebrating Holy Communion. It rests on the altar (on a stand or against a large pillow) and is used by a priest to guide the liturgy during the Holy Communion portion of the Eucharist.

missal stand An ornamental stand used to hold the Missal.

monstrance An ornamental object used to display a consecrated communion host. It could also be used to display a saintly relic.

palms Fronds of various species of palm tree, cut and used in celebration of Jesus's triumphal entry into Jerusalem on Palm Sunday. Afterward, palms are burnt and mixed with consecrated oil to produce ashes for Ash Wednesday the following year.

pascal candle (*Christ candle*) A large white candle, which may be decorated with a cross, the year of blessing, A (alpha) and Ω (omega), grains of incense, and other symbols of the resurrection. This is the first candle lit from the sacred fire of the Easter Vigil and burns through the fifty days of Easter. It represents the light of Christ returned to the world in his resurrection. It is often kept near the baptismal font and is lit for baptisms as well as during the Burial of the Dead, when it is carried in procession instead of a cross.

paten A plate, typically made of precious metal, used for holding bread during Holy Communion.

pyx A small ornamented container used to carry consecrated hosts to the sick, elderly, or home-bound.

reserved sacrament Consecrated bread and wine set aside after Holy Communion, usually in a tabernacle or aumbry, and saved for the sick or those who could not be present at worship.

sanctuary lamp (eternal flame, chancel lamp, everlasting light) Represents the presence of Christ, and remains lit at all times.

Sanctus bells (altar bells) A small bell or set of bells used to draw attention to specific moments during the Great Thanksgiving.

service book See *Missal* or *altar book*.

spoon (*for incense*) A metal spoon, shell, or other object used to transport incense from the boat to the thurible.

taper A thin candle. Some call the candle lighter a taper, used to light and extinguish altar candles.

tongs An instrument used to transport lit charcoal to a thurible.

thurible A metal container suspended from a set of chains holding burnt incense used to purify objects during a liturgical rite; also known as a *censer*.

torch A combustible light source used in processions; originally carried to just give light in darkened buildings; has come to represent bringing the fire of the Holy Spirit and the Light of Christ into a religious rite.

virge A staff, typically made of wood, carried by a verger; historically used to make way through crowds for a procession.

wafer See *host*.

Sanctuary lamp

PARAMENTS AND LINENS

Paraments are cloth or tapestry hangings or ornaments that decorate the space for worship, especially those hangings at the altar, pulpit, and lectern. The term is derived from the Latin, *parare*, "to decorate" or "prepare." A number of linens are also used on the altar and for use with the vessels, especially during Holy Communion. Acolytes may often be asked to bring any number of these to the altar from the credence table to the deacon or celebrant as they prepare the altar. A church's altar guild typically cares for these cloth materials.

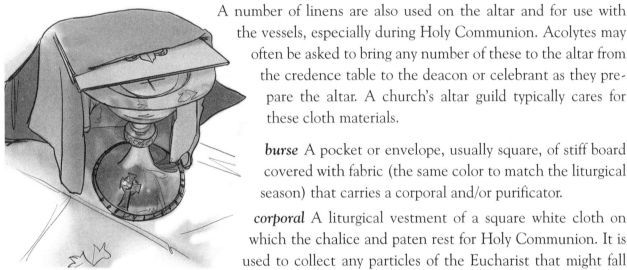

A view of a "dressed" chalice. The chalice is covered with a purificator with a paten resting on top (with a host on the paten). This is covered with a pall and veil. All of this is sitting on a corporal, which is spread out on an altar.

burse A pocket or envelope, usually square, of stiff board covered with fabric (the same color to match the liturgical season) that carries a corporal and/or purificator.

corporal A liturgical vestment of a square white cloth on which the chalice and paten rest for Holy Communion. It is used to collect any particles of the Eucharist that might fall during the prayer of consecration.

dossal Fabric or artwork hung behind the altar, against the east wall.

fair linen (*altar cloth*) A long piece of white linen or other fabric that covers the surface of the altar and hangs down the sides almost to the floor. It is typically embroidered with five crosses.

frontal A fabric, usually elaborately decorated and matching the seasonal color of the church year; it may cover the surface of the altar facing the congregation or all sides of the altar.

lavabo towel A linen used to dry the hands of the celebrant after washing, and before the beginning of the Great Thanksgiving.

pall A stiff, square cover that is placed over the chalice to keep objects from falling into the wine (such as insects).

pulpit fall A cloth, usually embroidered, that hangs from the front of the pulpit; typically matches the altar frontal and other vestments for each liturgical season.

purificator A linen cloth used to wipe, or purify, the chalice during Holy Communion.

veil A square piece of material of the same color for the church season (probably developed in the Middle Ages) to protect the chalice and paten while being carried to the altar. The burse rests on top of the veiled chalice.

MEMORIALS AND LOCATIONS

Every church is visually different from the outside as well as the inside. The liturgical space of each is filled with similar pieces of furniture even though the architectural style may be different. The most common arrangement is a cruciform space or a rectangular area with a center aisle with the chancel and altar at the east end. Since the 1960s and 1970s, altars that were built against the wall were either moved forward (closer to the congregation) or an additional freestanding altar was added so that the priest could stand behind it, facing the congregation during the liturgy.

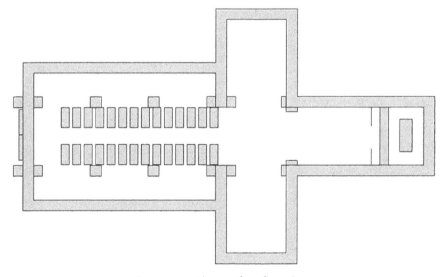

A sanctuary with a cruciform floor plan.

Some churches have pews; others have chairs that allow for flexibility in the worship space. Baptismal fonts are often located at the entrance to the nave while some churches have a separate baptistry area, constructed when baptism was seen as a private family affair instead of the main liturgy in the midst of the congregation like it is today. Colonial churches have a major focus on the pulpit, while Gothic-style churches (in the Anglo-Catholic tradition) are focused on the altar with accompanying decoration of reredos, triptychs, or rood screens. Choirs and organ may be placed behind the altar, to the side of the altar, or in the rear balcony. No two liturgical spaces are alike.

We have chosen to use the word *memorial* to describe the furniture and other physical objects that can be found within a church's worship space. Many vessels and objects are frequently donated by individuals who have been part of the parish in memory of a person or in thanksgiving of an event or person. Some may be engraved or have plaques placed upon them, noting the gift given "to the glory of God."

Acolytes should know the names of these locations and objects. They are key to where worship "moves" during the liturgy; acolytes often lead the way in processions to and from these locations.

A veiled chalice (center) on an altar with the Missal and missal stand (left) and Gospel Book (right) next to a eucharistic candle. Behind the altar is an altar cross (center) atop the tabernacle, which is flanked by two candles in front of a tryptic.

aisles Open spaces of the church which may run on the sides and/or through the center of the nave; the place where processionals occur while also providing access to the pews (or chairs) for the congregation to be seated.

altar A stone or wooden table at which the Holy Eucharist is celebrated.

altar rail A barrier made of wood, stone, or metal that separates the chancel from the sanctuary, or the chancel from the nave; kneelers (cushions) are often placed there to allow individuals to kneel for a blessing or to receive the Eucharist.

aumbry/ambry A small cupboard that holds the reserved sacrament in the wall or on a shelf apart from the altar in the sanctuary; see also *tabernacle*.

baptismal font The basin for the administration of the sacrament of Holy Baptism; a bowl-shaped piece of furniture used for baptism, specifically aspersions (sprinkling) and affection (pouring).

cathedra The chair or throne in which a bishop sits; also a symbolic presence representing the bishop in a congregation when not in use.

chancel The area of a church, usually raised up one or more steps, where the altar and seats for the clergy, eucharistic ministers, and acolytes are located.

chancel screen (or rood screen) An ornamental screen of wood or metal dividing the chancel from the nave.

credence table A side table in the chancel of the sanctuary, usually near or attached to the East Wall and in close proximity to the altar. It is used to hold the liturgical vestments and vessels before, during, or after Holy Communion.

The chancel of St. Matthew's Episcopal Church in Wilton, Connecticut, prepared for Palm Sunday.

kneeler A cushion or piece of furniture used to rest more comfortably in a kneeling position.

lectern A stand from which the lessons of the day are read; sometimes called an *ambo*; some lecterns are in the shape of an eagle, on whose outstretched wings a Bible rests. The eagle itself has many symbolic meanings, and can also represent the apostle John, writer of the Gospel of John.

narthex The vestibule or entryway before entering the nave, typically the west (opposite the altar on or near the east wall).

nave The area of the church where people gather to worship; it can also be viewed as the interior of a boat, with the ceiling appearing as the hull.

pew A long bench used to seat congregants in a sanctuary.

piscina A basin used specifically for washing communion vessels. The drain of the piscina, or sacrarium, leads to the earth below the church, and is not connected to typical plumbing; most often found in the *sacristy*.

A credence table prepared for the Eucharist with (back row, from right to left) a chalice with a purificator, cruet of water, two cruets of wine, (front row) lavabo bowl with towel, round bread box, cochlear spoon, square bread box, and pyx all on top of a fair linen.

Reredos

prayer desk A smaller piece of furniture that includes kneeler and lectern, used to lead liturgies or for private study.

pulpit A raised platform from which a sermon is preached and the Gospel may be read. Also called an *ambo*.

reredos An ornamental or artistic screen covering the wall behind the altar, typically depicting religious symbols and/or figures.

retable/altarpiece Any wooden, stone, or artistic structure placed on or immediately behind the altar. Used as decoration, and usually includes a painting, sculpture, or mosaic.

rood screen A richly carved wooden, metal, or stone screen that separates the nave from the chancel.

sacristy A room or rooms where the vessels, vestments, and other liturgical objects are kept; also an area where the clergy and lay minsters vest.

sanctuary The area of the church surrounding the altar; it means "sacred space."

sedilia The chair where the celebrant sits during the portion of the liturgy of the Word, often flanked by other chairs for the assisting altar party to sit.

tabernacle A decorative box, sometimes locked, containing the reserved sacrament. See *aumbry*.

transept An area that crosses the nave if the church has a cruciform shape; there may be pews or seating on the right or left in addition to the center portion of the nave.

triptych A picture, painting, or carving consisting of three panels, hinged together so as to be side by side, typically used as an altarpiece. See *retable*.

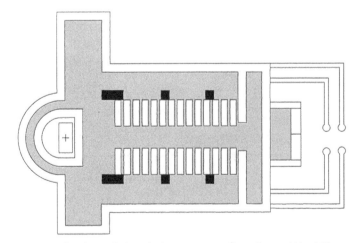

Another variation of what a sanctuary floor plan could look like.

CHAPTER SIX

Movements and Standards

WHETHER MANY OR FEW INDIVIDUALS lead worship, in actuality it is the work of the whole church. This includes a diversity of gifts used at the altar as well as those who come forth from the congregation. There are many roles played in liturgy, and each has its own function and purpose. A congregation with less than eighty people at weekly services may not have a full cadre of individuals to take on all the roles, including having more than one clergyperson or acolyte at a service. Larger congregations may have several clergy and dozens of volunteers to serve in each of the lay ministerial roles.

No matter how many or how few people there are to lead worship, it is important that all know who is responsible to do what, as well as how the movement of the liturgy will flow. This takes practice and clear communication between all involved. When each worship leader knows their role, liturgy can appear seamless; if not, it can lead to confusing pauses and fumbling that distract from the worship experience for all—including the congregation.

Here are the variety of roles and responsibilities that could be part of your congregation's service. Instead of being listed alphabetically, we have listed

A procession with (from front to back, right to left) verger, thurifer and boat bearer, crucifer, two torchbearers, banner bearer, choir, banner bearer, book bearer, deacon, two eucharistic ministers, celebrant, and bishop.

them in the order in which they typically enter the church in procession. We have also included the roles that members of the congregation take during the service. For our purposes, we can consider an acolyte in general terms as one who assists the ordained and licensed lay ministers at worship services, such as crucifer, torchbearer, server, thurifer, and others (denoted with a *).

In procession:

 verger Often called the "coordinator" of liturgy or master of ceremonies, this person assists in making sure the liturgy runs smoothly and often escort the procession, carrying a virge.

 thurifer Carries the thurible and uses it to cense areas of the sanctuary with incense.*

 boat bearer Carries the boat, presenting it appropriately for fueling the thurible.*

 crucifer Carries a processional cross.*

 torchbearer Carries a torch (or processional candle) in the processions of the liturgy.*

 choir A group of singers who provide musical leadership for congregational singing in worship; they may also sing special anthems or other musical offerings to enhance the liturgy.

 banner bearer Carries the church banner, or other appropriate artistic expression.*

server Any additional acolyte/s charged with assisting a bishop, priest, or deacon with the preparation of the altar for communion or any other capacity.*

 eucharistic minister A member of the congregation charged to represent Christ and his Church, and assist bishops, priests, and deacons in the administration of Holy Communion.

 **deacon** An ordained person charged with representing Christ and the Church, particularly as a servant to those in need, assisting bishops and priests in the proclamation of the Gospel, and administration of the sacraments; they would also carry the Gospel Book in processions. If there is not a deacon present, a lay minister or acolyte may perform the duty of **book bearer**.

 vested priests If there is more than one clergyperson assisting at the altar; such as one of the below who also have other roles in the liturgy:

subdeacon Historically a minor order of the church; typically a subdeacon fulfills a role in public liturgy when a deacon is not present.

preacher The person, typically ordained, charged with inspiring and making a connection between the biblical readings, the current situation of the world and our daily life, and the hope to be celebrated in the Eucharist to follow. (Another priest, the *celebrant,* or *bishop* may have this role.)

presider/celebrant The principal ordained presider of the Eucharist. If the service is other than Holy Eucharist, such as Morning Prayer, this person is called the *officiant.*

bishop's chaplain A person (a deacon if available) who assists the bishop during the liturgy by holding their crozier, mitre, prayer book, or other objects as requested; this is often a senior acolyte.*

bishop The apostle, chief priest, and pastor of a diocese. Bishops guard the faith, unity, and discipline of the whole church, proclaiming the Word of God, act in Christ's name for the reconciliation of the world and the building up of the church, and ordain others to continue Christ's ministry.

From the congregation:

lector A person who reads a lesson from the Hebrew Scriptures (Old Testament) or New Testament at the liturgy; sometimes call a *reader.*

intercessor A person who leads the Prayers of the People.

oblationer One or more persons from the congregation who bring the unconsecrated bread and wine (and water) at the time of the offertory to the altar.

usher A member of the congregation who assists seating congregants and collects the monetary offerings, presenting them at the time of the offertory during the service.

As we've previously noted, the ministry of an acolyte is one of silent presence. It involves moving seamlessly throughout the liturgy, assisting and serving in a variety of capacities, from leading the procession, to serving at the altar, to leading the final procession (or recession) at the end of the service. Each of the below listed words are actions that occur during The Holy Eucharist: Rite I or II. From congregation to congregation, the role of the acolytes will vary (* denotes a typical action in which an acolyte has a role to play or verbal response to make).

ACTIONS AND THEIR MEANINGS

ablutions A ritual of cleansing the communion vessels after communion either at the altar or credence table during the liturgy or in the sacristy after the service.

absolution A declaration of God's forgiveness of sins, administered by a priest or bishop, after the confession of sin is said by the congregation.

acclamation A loud and enthusiastic response of praise at the beginning of a service or during the eucharistic prayer.*

affusion The practice of baptizing a person by pouring water on the head.

benediction A prayer of blessing typically given at the end of a service.

bowing Lowering the head in a gesture of respect to a person, symbol, or concept. It is a momentary pause, as the eyes and head move toward the floor, then raised again. See also *solemn bow*.*

Bowing

censing The act of blessing the altar, clergy, and congregation with a thurible filled with burning, smoking incense by the celebrant (or in some cases the deacon or thurifer).*

chrismation Anointing a person with chrism (oil).

commendation The portion at the end of the Burial of the Dead (funeral liturgy) in which a person's body is commended to God.

concelebration A Eucharist at which other priests or bishops, vested according to their order, join the principal celebrant at the altar for the eucharistic prayer.

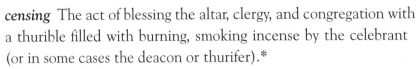

Censing

confirmation The rite in which we express a mature commitment to Christ, reaffirm our baptismal promises, and receive the laying-on-of-hands by a bishop.

consecration Declaring an object or space to be sacred.

dismissal The words said at the end of worship by a deacon or the celebrant sending the congregation out into the world.

elevation The act of raising the consecrated elements after the Words of Institution, at the conclusion of the Great Thanksgiving, or at the Invitation to Communion

eucharistic prayer The Great Thanksgiving, a prayer over bread and wine at Holy Communion.

Fraction The act of breaking the bread for communion.

genuflection Bending a knee (typically touching the right knee to the floor) to lower oneself in a sign of respect to the consecrated bread and wine (either in the tabernacle or ambry or on the altar).

gospel procession Walking the Gospel Book in a ceremonial manner to be amongst the congregation, so that the Gospel may be declared; usually led by a processional cross and torches.*

lighting (and extinguishing) candles Before worship, candles are lit on the altar and/or other locations, including the eucharistic candles or office lights, torches, and the Paschal candle (if during the Season of Easter, at baptisms, and burial rites); they are extinguished at the end of the service. Candles represent the light of Christ among us.*

kneeling Bending both knees to the ground as an expression of reverence, penitence, and respect.*

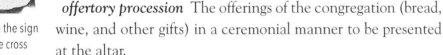

making the sign of the cross Tracing on one's forehead, chest, and shoulders the outline of the cross in the name of the Holy Trinity (Father—head, Son—chest, Holy Spirit—left shoulder to right shoulder). Conclude by clasping one's hands together at the waist.

offertory The act of receiving and presenting our time, talent, and treasure, along with the elements of bread and wine for Holy Communion.

offertory procession The offerings of the congregation (bread, wine, and other gifts) in a ceremonial manner to be presented at the altar.

Making the sign of the cross

procession A formal walk in or around a church or to a specific place led by a crucifer, torchbearers, and in some churches a thurifer, boat bearer, and/or banner bearer.*

recession A formal walk out of the church at the end of a service led by a crucifer, torchbearers, and others.*

serving In terms associated with the role of acolytes, this can be thought of as "fetching" and "carrying" vessels and other objects during the liturgy. It can be bringing the service book to the altar, bringing additional chalices, patens, or water to the altar, or any task that the clergy may ask an acolyte to do to assist.*

solemn bow The inclination of one's body from the waist as a sign of reverence. Hands can either be clasped at the waist or run down the legs to the knees. Think of it as looking at your shoes for a short period of time. This typically lasts longer than a "regular" bow described on page 44.*

stripping of the altars A rite carried out during the liturgy for Maundy Thursday in which all the linens and decorations of the church are removed or covered.*

veneration of the cross A rite carried out during the liturgy of Good Friday in which the clergy and congregation approach the cross with the intention of offering a gesture or moment of respect; in some places the veneration includes the act of kissing the foot of the cross.

vesting The act of putting on garments worn by liturgical leaders before the beginning of a service.*

washing of feet A rite carried out during the liturgy for Maundy Thursday in which the congregation washes each other's feet.

washing of hands Also known as *lavabo* (to wash), this is a ceremonial action in which the celebrant washes their hands before the Great Thanksgiving.*

Washing of hands

THE PRINCIPLES OF ETIQUETTE

Emily Post was an author whose name is synonymous with good manners and etiquette over seventy years ago. She began the Emily Post Institute in 1946, and the following are notes from an article titled, "The Principles of Etiquette":

> Etiquette . . . is made up of two parts. There are *manners*; lots of them, in fact. Books and webpages full of them! "Please" and "thank you," holding doors, chewing with our mouths closed, dressing appropriately, shaking hands—these are all manners. They are important because they give us confidence, allow our focus to be on the substance of our interactions, and they tell us what to do and what to expect others to do in return. Plus, they're nice.
>
> But etiquette also expresses something more, something we call "the principles of etiquette." Those are consideration, respect, and honesty. These *principles* are the three qualities that stand behind all the manners we have. They are timeless and cross-cultural boundaries, unlike manners, which can change over time and differ around the world.[27]

These are all traits that acolytes should strive to emulate when serving (and at other times too). How do these principles relate to ministry and being a Christian? These points can be good discussion starters at any acolyte training.

To **respect** another human being means to seek in that person a positive characteristic, skill, or quality and place a sense of worth on them for ourselves.

- "Will you strive for justice and peace among all people, and respect the dignity of every human being? *I will, with God's help.*" (Book of Common Prayer, p. 305)
- We strive to honor each other's time, talents, and personhood when we respect each other. Our actions best display our respect, or lack thereof. A respectful person prioritizes their commitments, prepares in dress, manner, and research for their commitments, and gives their full attention to the people or persons also engaged in those commitments.
- Respect is also about empathy. Empathy allows us to consider another person's point of view. When we are considerate we have a chance to grow and learn from the other. Being respectful, especially to people who have different opinions and experiences from us, is a chance to grow into a stronger person. The best rule for respect that Jesus gave us is, "Do to others as you would have them do to you" (Luke 6:31).

To be **honest** is to speak the truth in love. To speak the truth in love means to act and speak with kindness, gentleness, and sincerity.

- Honesty means keeping promises and commitment. An honest person means it when they say "yes" or "no."
- Empathy plays a role in honesty. The truth tempered in love can build another person up. With empathy we can understand how honesty can hurt and when it can be faithfully received.
- Honesty is also a quality of authenticity. We are strong enough to show others our true selves, warts and all.

---

27. Emily Post, "The Principles of Etiquette," The Emily Post Institute, accessed April 23, 2018, *http://emilypost.com/advice/the-principles-of-etiquette/.*

CHAPTER SEVEN

Building an Order

THE MINISTRY OF ACOLYTES IS MORE than what one sees during a worship service. Behind the scenes with mentors, clergy, and acolyte "masters" there are the responsibilities of calling individuals to this ministry, training, scheduling, recognition, the fitting of robes, and other minute details and administrative tasks. In some congregations, this leadership role is given to one person. In others, it involves levels of leadership with multiple people sharing the task. This should not be a burden, but a joy—sharing a passion and love for being able to serve God at God's altar.

Both Sharon and Roger served as acolytes as young people, and continue to mentor children, youth, and adults in the role as well as serve as an acolyte themselves from time to time. We believe that we are mentors first and foremost, learning alongside those who are novices as well as experienced.

ROGER'S STORY

I remember quite clearly the moment the picture was taken. In it, I am standing with four other acolytes on the steps of the Cathedral of St. Peter and St. Paul in Washington, DC. My goofy glasses and awkward stance belies a middle schooler firmly in the trenches of puberty. I look at the photo, still hanging at St. Thomas Episcopal Church in Weirton, West Virginia, and I am immediately transported back to that weekend in which we toured the Smithsonian, slept on a church floor, and most importantly: I, along with hundreds of other acolytes, processed in an enormous display of banners and robes through the cathedral for worship. That experience secured my identity as an acolyte. I was proud of the moment. I was proud of what I knew and how I was trained. I was passionate and committed to attaining the senior's cross that was offered at the end of the acolyte experience. Experiences and memories are powerful tools for guiding individuals along their personal path to self-actualization.

How do we create a ministry of formation with young people focused on service to the altar of Christ that is so powerful that it can only be described as a discernment process?

SHARON'S STORY

My first Sunday as an acolyte was Easter Sunday, along with Jill. I was sixteen; she was eighteen. We were the first females to serve at the altar in our parish. These were the days before women's ordination and before our current Book of Common Prayer (1979) was in church pews. Eucharist was not every Sunday, so we also served at Morning Prayer. But that Easter we celebrated Holy Communion (Eucharist was not part of our vocabulary yet) and the church was packed. One specific memory I have is that we were asked to wear our hair long and not tied back in a ponytail; we were to be seen for who we were—females serving at God's altar. I can still picture the training we had undertaken weeks and months before our "first" service. Knowing we were the first females to serve, our mentor made sure we knew everything so we could succeed. We processed up and down the church aisle holding the cross or flags (American and Episcopal—torches did not exist for us then) countless times, making sure our pace and stance was exact. Elbows up at 90-degree angles, hands in front of our faces, palms facing outward. We practiced handing flagons and cruets handles outward facing to the make-believe celebrant (who now happens to be a bishop), learning ablutions: wine—water—wine, lifting the alms basins high in front of the altar during the doxology, kneeling at the altar on a small square cushion (back and legs straight—no back rest, no slouching). We had to memorize the names of every type of linen, every vessel, and every action. It was hard work. We loved it.

LEADING A TRIBE

The best way to evolve the vital practice of acolyte ministry is to stop managing a program and begin leading a tribe that can evolve into an order. An order, according to Merriam Webster is "a group of people united in a formal way: such as a fraternal society 'the Masonic *Order*,' or a community under a religious rule; *especially* one requiring members to take solemn vows."[28] Likewise, Merriam Webster defines a tribe as "a group of persons having a common character, occupation, or interest."[29] Seth Godin defines it best:

> A tribe is a group of people connected to one another, connected to a leader, and connected to an idea. For millions of years, human beings have been part of one tribe or another. A group needs only two things to be a tribe: a shared interest and a way to communicate.[30]

---

28. *https://www.merriam-webster.com/dictionary/order.*

29. *https://www.merriam-webster.com/dictionary/tribe.*

30. Seth Godin, *Tribes: We Need You to Lead Us* (New York: Portfolio, 2008), audiobook.

We have witnessed tribes throughout history and follow them today. What is your favorite sports team? That is one of your tribes. Do a group of friends gather with you for game night? That is a tribe! Do you look forward to a weekly Bible study? That is your tribe as well.

Some Descriptors of Tribes

- Tribes are small but can be part of larger networks. All of the Steelers fans in Charlotte, North Carolina, are part of a tribe, but they are also part of the larger "Steeler Nation" tribe that stretches throughout the United States.

- Tribes are focused. They have a very specific reason for being and focus their attention to living into that reason with all their combined skill, energy, and resources.

- Tribes have a lifespan. They are born, grow strong, get larger, recede, decline, and pass away.

- Tribes are connected. They communicate to each other regularly and often.

- Tribes are incubators. When the healthy tribe has grown to a certain point, it will split into smaller tribes, each with their own identity and purpose.

How might we inspire others to join a tribe so that we may rebrand acolyte ministry as a place where seekers gather and discover God's presence in their life through service, discipline, and reverence? Roger's tribe at Good Shepherd in Augusta, Georgia, believes that serving God's altar is a chance to be "altared" from the inside out. It is a supernatural experience that contains whispers of dreams and calls to action. It is the lynchpin that holds together a young person's Christian identity and (re)presents the spiritual blessings and gifts bestowed on them by God.

In the Bible, Jacob blesses his sons, making them a family of tribes: all these are the twelve tribes of Israel, and this is what their father said to them, blessing each one of them with a suitable blessing (Gen. 49:28). Everyone had a blessing, a purpose, and a role to play according to their blessing. A tribe will help our children and youth find their place in our church and community.

WHY TRIBES ARE IMPORTANT

It used to be enough that one declared themselves a Christian; through that identity they were brought into the Christian tribe and given a role. But it also used to be that you could achieve "the American Dream" by just enrolling in and supporting the mass culture. It used to be that all church youth workers had to do was show up, because there wasn't much to compete with for the hearts and souls of our young people. The world, however, is changing, and while what used to be is gone, what was before might be coming back.

Mass culture is the sum of our media, rules, and expectations that we receive from others and the culture around us. It defines the unwritten law of appropriate life choices and expectation. It is also "the world" as opposed to "the kingdom of heaven" we read about in scripture. In the twenty-first century, we are witnessing our mass culture break apart and fragment into smaller, tribal groupings. Today, you find your tribe and your culture by defining your individual identity and seeking similar persons with which to be affiliated, not by falling in line with the mass culture and doing what is expected. We live in the age of 100 percent customization, in which people find their comfort and community in a system defined by tribal groupings built on shared experience, worldview, and opinion.

The world in which our young people are growing up is fractured. Our world is the echo chamber in which they are formed and through which their attention is sought. If there is not a call to join a tribe of believers, then our young people will never become believers. By approaching our youngest with an invitation to join the ranks of acolytes or any other ministry (our tribe), we are building a community of seekers who share one common vision: being nearer to God. This is how we build a tribe:

1. We identify the culture in which we work and how it is different from and similar to the mass culture.
2. We design a compelling vision of a new world, and present that vision by means of a statement—a way of life we choose to follow.
3. We accept our responsibility as the tribal leader and develop a process to oversee the tribe we are attempting to build.

4. We use shared experiences to commit young people (and adults) to this vision of the world as it is described in our manifesto. We talk about creating a personal and program mission statement as a way of life in the appendix.
5. We empower tribe members to become leaders themselves that start their own movements to form new tribes.

This is how Jesus built a tribe, which started a movement, which changed the world.

GROWING A TRIBE 1: IDENTIFY YOUR CULTURE

He left Nazareth and made his home in Capernaum. (Matt. 4:13)

After his baptism and temptation, Jesus went right to work, and he knew where he wanted to be. He consciously traveled to an environment in which lived a specific culture, and once he was comfortable in that culture, he began the work of calling disciples into his tribe. It is important to understand the culture in which you are operating this ministry, because each culture has different rules and expectations. The use of the term *culture* does not describe the customs, history, and artistic expressions of a place or people. It describes the sum behavior and attitudes of a small group of people, a tribe, within the larger context of a church community. These three culture descriptions are inspired by the work of Seth Godin in *Tribes: We Need You to Lead Us*.

Reactionary Cultures

A *reactionary* culture relies almost entirely on instinct and intuition. Many smaller ministries run in a reactionary culture. Typical norms of the acolyte program that react to the world are:

- Making up schedules month by month, or not using schedules.
- Training students when we have time, or when we have enough interested people to make it worthwhile.
- Scrambling to fill spots for people who do not show up when scheduled.
- Very little communication of standards, expectations, and affirmations. People are expected to "just know how we do it here."

The culture ruled by *reaction* produces tribes without leaders, or very part-time leaders. Time to organize and focus the mission of the tribe has not been given priority, and the group does not typically have a common vision to work toward. Somewhere, most likely in the distant past, someone took over leading the tribe believing that the purpose of the tribe's existence was just that: to exist. Jumping to the present activity of the tribe, everything is now done at the last minute, and most decisions are made in *reaction* to whatever challenge presents itself. *Reacting* to challenges typically works because we intuitively know what to do to survive social interactions.

We think there is not time to grow a big, complicated program, so we just wing it, usually with one person who *manages* the activity of the ministry, but who doesn't actually *lead* the people through it. In a *reactionary* acolyte ministry, the participants decide whether or not they take their ministry seriously. The typical, unspoken vision in this culture is: "We all serve. Take your turn on the schedule, get through the service with minimal embarrassment, and thank you for giving us your time."

Responsive Cultures

Another culture is one where the tribe has evolved from *reacting* to developing *responses* so that it is ready for most challenges. To *respond* well to any given scenario you need a minimum of two elements: time to think, and previous training. Most "well run" acolyte programs operate at this level. Typical norms of the acolyte program functioning in this culture include:

- A recurring or regular schedule that is known to all, written far enough in advance that no one is surprised when it is their turn to serve at the altar.
- Fixed training regimens are in place, often with a manual, and there is some accountability to the expectation written down and expressed therein.
- Some form of affirmation and/or debriefing system is in place that recognizes the effort of servers as valuable enough to express gratitude and feedback.

Ministries established in and governed by *responses* acknowledge that competition exists in the world, and because of competition, expectations must be communicated clearly to all people in the ministry. *Responsive* environments can include many of the elements from the *reactionary* environment but has taken time to develop a system to respond to stressors and uncertainties that regularly present themselves to the members of the tribe. Ministries that *respond* to their participants' needs typically produce leaders from within organically. That is, when a person presents themselves for leadership, we *respond* with further training and a higher expectation of time and expertise.

Initiating Cultures

A culture that has evolved beyond *responding* and has invested energy into building experiences is one that *initiates*. To be an *initiator*, a ministry must be imaginative and focus on creating systems and processes that *respond* to the needs of its audience and *reacts* to challenges *before* they present themselves. People within the tribe are seen as an individual client with their own needs and goals. Typical norms of the acolyte program that responds to the world are:

- Acolytes are empowered to lead because they are authentically called to serve, have enough information to feel competent in their sacred duty, and do this work in a real community of likeminded ministers.

- There are very clear expectations, with encouragement to evolve or strengthen the expectations when individuals feel the need to do so. The group collectively defines the identity and boundaries of the tribe.
- The tribe's vision lies beyond the immediate purpose of self-perpetuation. Acolytes in this environment know that serving is not the end; it is the means by which a relationship with God is built.
- The processes that define this environment encourage an individual to initiate responses in other parts of their life. They are given tools and support to be initiators outside the acolyte ministry.

A culture that *initiates* a relationship between its members and God so that they may in turn effectively engage the outside world is a culture that believes itself to be an incubator. It produces tribe members who are ready to go where God leads them to initiate their own tribes with the knowledge and experience the environment has given to them. The members are truly empowered to "go and do likewise."

GROWING A TRIBE 2: DESIGN A COMPELLING VISION

To create an environment that empowers individuals to take on leadership and build tribes, you need a leader with a vision. In Matthew 4:17–20, we hear a most brilliant vision from an obviously inspired leader. Jesus's vision is simple: "Repent, for the kingdom of heaven has come near." Jesus proclaims that message and challenges two individuals to live into the vision with him. He used a simple, life-changing phrase: "Follow me, and I will make you fish for people." These verses provide us with an example of how to present our vision for the world:

- Repent. An examination of our life is always a good starting point. Are you content? What is missing?

- For the kingdom of heaven is near. Declare what it is that is within reach that may bring you joy and contentment.

- Come. He starts with a challenge. A call to action.

- Follow me. Jesus identifies himself as the leader. He is asking for trust and respect, so that the disciples do not doubt who the leader is.

- And I will send you out. Here, Jesus is appealing to the disciples' dreams: to be important, to be sent, to be powerful, to be leaders.

- To fish for people. Jesus wraps up his vision by affirming the disciples' identity as fishermen. He is empowering them to be who they are, but bigger versions of themselves.

Our vision of what acolytes are doing at every worship service should be just as powerful and appealing but can only be delivered through the leader. No amount of media or nonhuman communication can spark passion and build loyalty better than a human being standing before you saying, "Come, follow me."

The leader must do some work before they begin to express their vision to tribe members. They must clearly define a vision of the world as it would look if their tribe of acolytes were to come closer to God.

- What is your call to action? What challenge can you present to your acolytes that inspire them?

- What are the goals you can set in place that if acolytes follow you, they will meet? What will happen if they follow you?

- What education do these acolytes need to have in order to be sent out into the world with competence and authenticity?

- What impact will this ministry have on the world because your acolytes have participated in it?

Your vision is the driving force behind the acolyte ministry. A vision can be handed down from the church itself, from clergy or leadership, or from within yourself. It should be simple but convey a new or different environment from the current one you operate in.

Roger's vision for the acolyte ministry at Church of the Good Shepherd is:

Join me as we discover how to see the real and living God that presents in and amongst us every Sunday. Grow stronger as we come closer to Christ's altar with poise and confidence, so that others are moved by our presence and ministry. Use your powerful imagination and creativity to transform your hour on Sunday to something wonderful, so that God may do wonderful acts through you to those whom you meet.

The vision does not have to be the mission of the ministry or a reflection of the church's ministry. This is the tribal leader's vision, one that is tailored to you and is authentic, coming from your experience. This statement helps the leader to set goals, boundaries, and measurements of success along the process of growing the tribe. Take a moment to identify your vision. You can't lead without it, and without it you won't know in what direction you are leading your tribe.

GROWING A TRIBE 3: ACCEPT RESPONSIBILITY AS THE TRIBAL LEADER

In a battle between two ideas, the best one doesn't necessarily win. No, the idea that wins is the one with the most fearless heretic behind it.[31]

"[Come,] follow me, and I will make you fish for people" is the single sentence that defined the vision that puts into motion a series of momentous events that evolved into the church of today. Because of the utterance of this one sentence, two human beings evolved into a tribe, transformed a tribe into a movement, and became a global phenomenon that is currently estimated to have 2.4 billion followers. Jesus truly was fearless in his vision. No one who followed the mass culture of the time would leave their family trade to follow an itinerant rabbi.

Your vision is just as important, but it will get nowhere unless you are able to lead fearlessly. To be able to lead fearlessly, you will need to be content with what you are leading. In his book, Sebastian Junger identified that

human beings need three basic things in order to be content: they need to feel **competent** at what they do; they need to feel **authentic** in their lives; and they need to feel **connected** to others. These values are considered "intrinsic" to human happiness and far outweigh "extrinsic" values such as beauty, money and status.[32]

A leader has a vision and a plan that gives people those three things: competency, authenticity, and connectivity. Creating an environment that initiates all of those attributes in people is the key to creating a ministry that "altars" lives and forms disciples that can then go out to initiate new tribes that begin the process again. This is your ultimate responsibility as the tribal leader: to secure authenticity, build competency, and create community.

Secure Authenticity

Christian formation often speaks about authenticity. It is the key to building relationships. It is a

---

31. Seth Godin, *Tribes: We Need You to Lead Us* (New York: Portfolio, 2008), 1.
32. Sebastian Junger, *Tribe: On Homecoming and Belonging* (New York: Hatchett Book Group, 2016), 22. Emphasis added.

foundational element of a relationship that must be present in order to build trust, commitment, and rapport. The only real way to be authentic is to be honest with yourself. If you are not energized by the concept of leading a ministry, then why are you leading it? If your passion is not stoked watching acolytes lead worship, then why are you knee deep in this work? The issue of authenticity is addressed by simply asking yourself:

1. What is my role? Am I a leader or a follower? Pick a role and run with it. It is ok to say, for example, "I'm not a leader, I don't have a vision for this ministry, but I'm a great organizer and I can keep this together until a person with a vision is presented to us."

2. How do my gifts and skills make this tribe stronger? Be yourself; use your experience and gifts. Use what you know.

Build Competency

Humans don't mind hardship, in fact they thrive on it; what they mind is not feeling necessary. Modern society has perfected the art of making people not feel necessary.[33]

There are three steps to ensuring your acolyte tribe is competent in their role as worship leaders:

1. Knowing the Holy Eucharist Rite II (or whichever liturgy you are leading as an acolyte) inside and out.

2. Repetition of the service and actions enough that it becomes instinctual.

3. Mentoring another person so that they can be competent as well. Teach others what you know.

This is where the concept of the "lead" acolyte comes in. The idea of the lead is that one person, a mature seeker who has professed a call to lead others, has spent more time and energy becoming competent in this role, and has repeated it enough that they are able to teach younger acolytes how to do it well. You will find an outline for a training retreat for leads and other acolytes in the appendix.

Create Community

Modern society has perfected the art of making people not feel necessary.[34]

The plague of our age is loneliness. Loneliness is a spiritual condition that can only truly be answered by connectivity with the Body of Christ. To connect our people to each other, we need both competency and authenticity. We need to know the people of our tribe: to understand their desires, dreams, and hopes. We are then able to connect them to others in a way that is unique to each person, so that every person in our tribe feels necessary. We can only do this if we know who they are, and if we are authentic in how we initiate conversation and responsibility within the environment.

---

33. Sebastian Junger, *Tribe: On Homecoming and Belonging* (New York: Hatchett Book Group, 2016), xvii.
34. Ibid.

There are three common building blocks that create teams and community:

- Trust. Without trusting each other's limits and strengths, it is hard to move a team forward. Trusting others begins with trusting oneself and trusting oneself begins with knowing oneself. Personality trait study, strengths, spiritual gifts, weaknesses, mutual review, affirmative inquiry are all tools to help people to know their gifts and skills and develop plans for utilizing them in the community.

- Communication. Ropes course and initiative games are brilliant tools to develop communication. The methods of communication need to be established at the beginning of tribal formation and then used consistently. Sending printed material home after a training along with an e-mail blast and a group text should be standard practice and following it all up in person is essential. No one ever complained about overcommunication.

- Perseverance. Living in community is messy. People will become offended, feelings will get hurt, and mistakes will be made. That is a given. What is not a given is how we respond to those moments when they arise. Be willing to persevere past any embarrassment or hurt in order to sustain relationships. Reconciliation is underutilized in many communities and is something we should be modeling with

and to others. We need perseverance to do the hard work of understanding, compromising, and growing with others in Christ's name in all that we do.

GROWING A TRIBE 4: SHARE EXPERIENCES TO COMMIT ACOLYTES TO A VISION

Contemporary identities are composed of experiences, representations, and everyday emotions. Modern tribalism is ephemeral, with fluid boundaries, and temporary networks.[35]

Memory is powerful. It defines our experiences and shapes our worldview. When we participate in a powerful moment, it carries an equally powerful memory that goes forward with us throughout our lives. But we are not computers. Memories are not video stills that record exact details of the experience. Even though we remember key points of the experience, it is still just a representation of that moment, not a recording. The memory then triggers an emotional reaction as well, so what we experience when we take a trip down memory lane is a complete spiritual moment of emotion, representation, and images of a dream. This human mechanism can be a positive process, as we

---

35. Michael Maffesoli, *The Time of the Tribes: The Decline of Individualism in Mass Society* (London: Sage Publications, 1996), 76.

revisit our wedding day or the birth of a child, or it could be painful and bring back the experience of trauma.

Game developers know this process well, and they know the mechanics of the brain to make fantasy a reality. While a person plays a video game, their heart rate increases, they sweat, they get nervous, joyous, miserable, and more as they seem to "live" the digital reconstruction on the screen. Role-playing games and some board games have proven to have the same effect. When you are imagining surviving a zombie apocalypse, your brain actually responds as if you are in the real apocalypse!

A new educational trend uses the term *gamification*. This is using principles of psychology and game design to create experiences though which people can deal with issues, such as painful memories, or learn concepts and processes from their standard classroom. Escape rooms have become popular for just this reason; they give people the experience of a high-pressure adventure in a completely safe environment. Virtual reality technology is improving at light speed and has the same effect. A person engaged in these "games" has the same biological reaction as people who experience the same moments in reality. Our fighter pilots and astronauts spend time in simulators, "practicing" for the real mission.

Christian formation is "practicing" alongside young people in order to guide and teach them what they need to mature into one who glorifies God, is a blessing to others, and brings joy to themselves. In the past, the Church has followed a traditional course in educating young people to prepare for adulthood by passing on facts and information we felt they needed to know. More and more, we are learning that their "experience" of God in and through church defines their trajectory far more completely than what they "know" about God. The great news is that our liturgy framed by the Book of Common Prayer has proven to be a valid and powerful tool for a community to have an experience of God in worship. In the liturgy, the music could be off, or a sermon could miss the mark, or a series of prayers could be rushed or muttered or forgotten, and people could still leave church having a memory of the experience of God.

How do we use the aggregation of gamification and a proven liturgical experience to shape our students for their ministry at the altar? How do we tap into their shared experiences, and provide them with memories of positive worship experiences that they will carry all their lives? The key shift here is to stop training those to serve *in* worship and begin guiding them in having an experience *of* worship. The most efficient, cost effective, and powerful way to present these formative experiences is by presenting them as retreats. Designing and presenting a retreat provides some benefits over other methods. They are:

- By gathering outside everyone's normal environment, the normal prejudices and worldview they unconsciously carry with them are removed.

- Joining together in a new environment, or into an existing environment in a new way, a response is triggered from them that whatever happens in this space is somehow more powerful than the mundane world of everyday life.
- The lessons taught through experience do not need to be learned or memorized, because they are assimilated into memory and become tied to emotions and representations, which have more power than recalling facts or concepts.
- In one overnight retreat, the leader of this "tribe" will have more face-time with their acolytes than they would in a one-hour session meeting weekly for two months. Compare the effort of maintaining a two-month workshop series versus an overnight retreat. Compare the cost of those two options.

We are made to be tribal people: close knit, small groups, sharing resources, and protecting each other. What better place than church is there to experience that without the trauma of war? What is a better way to build a new generation of engaged, compassionate, creative voices than by offering them an annual shared experience of Christian community?

BE A CATALYST FOR LEARNING

Today's teacher, mentor, or leader does not need to be the "sage of the stage." How many times at rehearsals, practices, and in classrooms, do students mutter, "How does this even help me? How is this useful to me? What difference does this really make?" While the often quoted proverb, "Train children in the right way, and when old, they will not stray" (Prov. 22:6) is traditional wisdom, it goes deeper. Too often we strive to teach and raise young people in the way they should go without giving context or making a connection with something deeper in their personal life. Leaders should strive to be the catalyst for learning, not the source of it, and prepare an environment that is conducive to learning. By setting goals for what is to be accomplished, creative ways for experiencing and absorbing new information can be developed, knowing who the intended audience is.

The leader as a catalyst can present knowledge through games, experiences, and most importantly, questions. When you offer questions that allow participants to debrief the experience they just had, each can be their own judge of how the material is useful in life. We cannot force-feed a potential altar server the importance of standing respectfully next to the Lord's altar at communion, but we can give them an experience of it and process it with them afterward in such a way that they can judge for themselves its value. As previously noted, you will find an outline of an acolyte training retreat in the appendix. Using this model, you can build a tribe of acolytes who have a shared experience of the power of this ministry that they will carry the rest of their lives.

At its heart, worship is our collective remembrance and living through the life, death, and resurrection of Christ. That is an experience that needs to be replayed over and over for us. If we update our processes of teaching acolytes how to engage the Christian story through worship, they can do so with all of their considerable skill and spiritual gifts.

EMPOWER TRIBE MEMBERS TO BECOME LEADERS

As the Church, we seem to forget the difference between empowerment for ministry and burdening the laborer. How many times does our idea of involving the youth group in an event translate into their putting away the chairs or cleaning up the mess? Sometimes we put students into leadership positions when they are not authentically engaged, competent enough to fulfill our expectations of them, or surrounded by a support group. What this leads to is a traumatic experience, not a formative one. Mentoring and leadership involves the raising up of new leaders for ministry. Whatever they may be called—head acolyte, lead, prior, or prioress—an experienced senior acolyte is a vital component to this ministry. The name is not as important as the duty, which includes:

- Accepting a call and formally responding to the church as a minister by means of rituals, vows, or other commitment ceremony.

- Becoming adept and competent at leading worship, which includes understanding why we do what we do in worship, what order it happens in, and what needs to be done to make this experience better for the worshiping community.

- Claiming a responsibility for the people in the pews, knowing that the work of the worship team is truly a team-based effort. Clergy cannot manifest a powerful worship experience by themselves, and it requires every person at the altar to be focused, ready, and willing to receive what God is offering us in worship.

- Claiming responsibility for their tribe. It does not matter if you have three acolytes or seventy-three. That group of human beings must understand that someone is looking out for them, caring for them, and working hard for them. Breaking your corps of acolytes into small groups of four, eight, or whatever number suits your typical Sunday needs, with an attached lead acolyte is an equation for a tight knit community of supportive and engaged people.

- With training, clear communication, engaged participation, and the development of new leaders, the burden of leadership falls to a team, and not only to the tribal leader and mentor. The mentors then become the catalyst of ministry, not the driving force of it. We give room for God to do what God always does: create life.

CHAPTER EIGHT

An Acolyte's Way of Life

I pray that you, being rooted and established in love, may have power, together with all the Lord's holy people, to grasp how wide and long and high and deep is the love of Christ, and to know this love that surpasses knowledge—that you may be filled to the measure of all the fullness of God. (Eph. 3:17-19, NIV)

AT THE 79TH GENERAL CONVENTION of the Episcopal Church, Presiding Bishop Michael Curry called the Episcopal Church to join him in *The Way of Love: Practices for a Jesus-Centered Life.*

Turn: Pause, listen, and choose to follow Jesus

Learn: Reflect on scripture each day, especially on Jesus' life and teachings

Pray: Dwell intentionally with God daily

Worship: Gather in community weekly to thank, praise, and dwell with God.

Bless: Share faith and unselfishly give and serve

Go: Cross boundaries, listen deeply, and live like Jesus

Rest: Receive the gift of God's grace, peace, and restoration[36]

As we build our tribe and support the spiritual development of our acolytes, inviting each to follow a way of life and create their own personal vision (as well as create one for yourself and your ministry) will tie everything together. It brings the head and heart together with intentionality, reinforcing this ministry as one that is life-giving and not simply a task to show up and perform during worship.

---

36. "The Way of Love," The Episcopal Church, accessed July 20, 2018, *https://www.episcopalchurch.org/way-of-love.*

CRAFTING A PERSONAL WAY OF LIFE

A personal manifesto expresses your core values and beliefs, what you stand for, what you are not willing to be compromised by, and how you intend to live your life. A rule of life is a commitment to live your life in a particular way—created with prayer and discernment. It is an intentional pattern of spiritual disciplines, such as prayer and reading the Bible, which provides structure and direction to live a holy life. In partnering with God and understanding the gifts that God has given you, you create a pattern to follow every day, acknowledging the God made you and the beliefs you hold are inscribed on your heart.

St. Benedict's Rule of Life is perhaps the most famous and is still followed by many today. It establishes a way of life rooted in the gospel and grounded in principles of charity, humility, stability, and faithfulness. Communities that follow a Rule of Life together often say, "It says 'this is who we are, this is our story'; and it reminds us of those things God has put on our hearts."

Begin by Crafting a Purpose Statement

- What is your current goal?
- What do you believe?
- By what Rule of Life do you choose to live?[37]

Declare Your Beliefs

- What do you seek?
- What are three to five core concepts or foundational beliefs that you would like to keep in front of yourself at all times?

Tools

Define the skills, attributes, character strengths, experiences, and spiritual gifts that help you to be who you are.

- What are you passionate about?
- What did your ten-year-old self love to do?

---

37. Some examples of a Rule of Life: The Rule of St. Benedict, *http://www.osb.org/rb/text/toc.html*; the Society of St. John the Evangelist (SSJE), *http://www.ssje.org/growrule/*; The Rule of St. Augustine, *https://augustinians.squarespace.com/s/The-Rule-of-St-Augustine.pdf*; The Order of the Ascension, *http://www.orderoftheascension.org/rule-of-life* (all accessed May 31, 2018).

- What makes you feel alive when you do it?
- In what environment do you thrive?

Short Terms

List your three to five short-term goals that are quintessential to your current happiness.

1. Keep them short, as few words as possible.
2. Choose attainable goals in short time frames: three months, six months, one year.
3. Choose one goal that is so audacious that only God can help you truly attain it.

Your Rule (or Way) of Life

- A statement of self-assessment. Who are you? What is your greatest strength? What is your greatest weakness?
- What disciplines do you choose to follow regularly? Explain how you will practice them. What are two to three guidelines
  you can set that will help you stay close to your rule?
- Express your form of accountability. How will you judge your ability to commit and grow through these practices?

Accountability

- When will you reevaluate this way of life?
- Who will you share this with, if anyone?
- Can you name someone who will help you make this a reality?

Roger offers his personal manifesto as an example of what one might look like. In the appendix you will find a template in which you can help your acolytes, mentors, leaders, and parents to create their own way of life, perhaps as part of their ministry of being an acolyte. And don't forget Presiding Bishop Michael Curry's call to *The Way of Love: Practices for a Jesus-Centered Life*.[38]

---

38. *https://www.episcopalchurch.org/way-of-love*

ROGER'S MANIFESTO

Purpose Statement

My life is my ministry: to my family, my church, and my students. My ministry is led by the spirit, not by wounds—not mine, nor the church's, nor my clients. My song is my art, and my art will glorify God in all ways.

I seek:	• Comfort	• The health of my	• Belonging	• Creativity
	• Faith	whole self	• Family	• Union

Rules of Life

- I will be a trailblazer, and one must have equal parts of courage and faith, grit, and stupidity to be a trailblazer.
- I will organize this "thing" once. I will design it and make it as strong as I can. Do it right the first time and anticipate the tripwires that may make this project stumble later.
- Do what needs to be done now, not a year from now. If not me, who? If not now, when?
- People judge by outward appearance, God judges the heart.

Short Terms

1. Attain equilibrium, but only for today.
2. Publish the book.
3. Build the school
4. Be your own boss.

Accountability

- If this gets in the book, a whole lot of people just got to know me better.
- Read this every day, first thing.
- Share with Fran, ask for her help.

My Tools

- <u>Gamification.</u> Use elements of challenge and play and story in nongamer contexts.

- <u>Experiences.</u> Teach me and I will forget. Show me and I will learn. Involve me and I will understand.

- <u>Collaboration.</u> Coming together is a beginning. Keeping together is a process. Working together is success.

- <u>Faithfulness.</u> Do something you've never done to get something you've never had.

- <u>Safety.</u> "Cynefin" (Welsh). A place where one feels they ought to live and belong, where nature around you feels right and welcoming.

CRAFTING A PROGRAM MISSION STATEMENT

We might also think of this as your purpose statement for your church's acolyte ministry. It follows the same pattern as creating a personal way of life but is broad and should be compatible with your parish mission or vision statement. State your program's title and clearly articulate its mission. Then broadcast it widely to all in your congregation, even beyond those participating in the ministry of acolytes.

Background

- What supporting information do you need to express the ministry's mission?
- What is "the main thing" that people must realize in order to understand your ministry's mission?
- How does your ministry fit into the ministry of the larger organization?

Goals of the Ministry

- Narrow your focus down to the top two or three goals you would like to achieve this calendar or program year.
- Wordsmith your goals to be simple, powerful, and completely clear.
- Make your goals measurable so that you may judge a year from now whether you have made progress or not.

Expectations of the Ministry

Acolyte Commitment

1. Who does this ministry include?
2. What is this ministry accomplishing, specifically?
3. When should participants be present?
4. Where does this ministry gather?
5. Why is it important for a person to commit to this ministry?

Parental Involvement

- Who is in charge here?
- What can a parent do to positively influence success?

- When should a parent step forward, and when should they let their child lead?
- Where can a parent help the ministry most effectively?
- Why is this ministry vital to your child's Christian formation?

Spiritual Growth and Development

- In what three to five ways will this ministry positively impact the acolyte's Christian formation?

How Is This Ministry Organized?

- Who is the leader?
- How is authority distributed?
- How are acolyte leaders empowered?
- Drawings are always helpful.
- Communicate visually as much as possible.

SAMPLE PROGRAM MISSION STATEMENT[39]

Altar Servers at Good Shepherd

Leading students to be the best versions of themselves by experiencing the Risen Christ in worship.

I serve the Lord's table
Good Shepherd Student Ministry

The altar is the focal point of our church, symbolizing Jesus's constant presence among us. It is at the altar that we offer up our prayers of thanksgiving for the great love that has been given to us in the life, death, and resurrection of Jesus. It is at the altar that we make intercession for friends or family, for the community, and the world. It is at the altar that we ask the Holy Spirit to receive our offering of bread and wine and give back to us the real presence of Jesus. Therefore, it is with reverence and respect that we serve our Lord at his altar.

Our Ministry Is Three-Fold

1. We lead worship as part of a team. As an altar server, our place at the altar and presence in the chancel of the church puts us in a role of leadership that we share with the clergy and other adult leaders. Our presence must be respectful and humble. It should not distract from the mystery shared with us at each worship service.

2. We serve God and serve God's people as worship progresses through the movements of the liturgy. The liturgy directs the people of God to encounter the living God as revealed in Holy Communion, scripture, and the witness of our brothers and sisters.

3. We are disciples wherever we go and must be mindful that our example bears witness to Jesus and his commandment to "Love others as I have loved you."

Altar Server Commitment

- Attend an annual training event. We will offer two: August and January.
- Communicate with your lead prior to your assigned service about your availability.
- Arrive fifteen minutes before your assigned service.
- Authentically engage in this ministry.
- Display competency in the language and movements of our liturgy.
- Connect with others in our community.

---

39. This is a sample used at Church of the Good Shepherd in Georgia. Copyright ©2018 The Reverend Robert D. Fain. Used with permission.

Parental Involvement

- The parent is the primary catechist of a child.
- A child cannot participate by themselves; they need your help to arrive on time and be sufficiently rested and ready to serve.
- Responsibility and reliability are character traits that we wish to develop in our acolytes.
- This is a family commitment.
- Share in the debrief process with your child.

Spiritual Growth and Development

Serving the altar is a sacred privilege and worship is a joyful event.

We believe this is accomplished in three specific ways:

Community: A Team Experience

Acolytes are currently scheduled individually to serve. Acolytes are grouped in teams of five to seven and are scheduled to serve at God's altar on a rotating basis. This creates a stronger sense of belonging for each acolyte and encourages students to connect with others of our community.

Authenticity: Servant Leadership

Students who complete training and wish to be recognized as lead acolytes will lead their teams by making assignments, encouraging younger students, and making the acolyte experience more rewarding for each student by developing the understanding that all are called to serve in their own way.

Competency: Excellence and Spiritual Growth by Debriefing

Teams will debrief with each other and an adult leader after each service, offering insights into how they performed as a team and sharing about their worship experience and response to scripture, liturgy, the sermon, and Holy Communion.

Leading and Serving Roles

Guild Master

1. Schedule and implement training for leads, servers, and bearers.
2. Create an annual calendar using the team-based, student-led lead system.
3. Mentor students to experience a more meaningful service and oversee the debriefing process.

<u>Assistant Guild Master</u>

1. Assist in teaching at trainings for guilds.
2. Assist guild master in managing annual calendar.
3. Mentor acolytes to create a more meaningful service experience and oversee the debriefing process.

<u>Guild (Parent)</u>

1. Maintain the acolyte vestments.
2. Mentor acolytes to create a more meaningful service and oversee the debriefing process.
3. Assist with trainings and special events.

Guilds

- Exercise responsibility for five to seven bearers and servers, from which they build a team for their assigned service by text, phone, and/or e-mail.
- Fill any role of the worship team.
- Understand aspects of the theology, liturgy, history, etiquette, and choreography of the worship service.
- Express a call to this ministry of leadership.
- Lead worship processions.
- Mentor bearers during the service, including but not limited to: when to move, when to refocus, and how to participate.
- Understand aspects of the liturgy, etiquette, and choreography of the worship service.
- Demonstrate spiritual maturity consistent with these expectations.
- Carry symbols of the liturgy into worship.
- Practice the ministry of presence during worship.
- Open to sixth grade and older.

You will find a template in the appendix to help you craft your acolyte program manifesto.

Making This Work

The following pages contain documents that you may copy and use for training your acolytes. You may find they need adjusting to your own context depending on your church's liturgical style and needs of your youth (and adults). The previous chapters will aid you (the leader or mentor) in learning the fine details and terminology that you can use as a reference. You may desire to take some of this appendix material and develop your own acolyte handbook specific to your congregation.

These appendices are organized in chronological order with regard to building or redesigning an acolyte program. Think of each document as a step in the process:

1. **The Ministry of the Acolyte:** a description and list of expectations for those discerning a call to this ministry.
2. **Crafting Your Way of Life:** A template to create your personal rule of life as the ministry leader and present it to supporters as a manifesto.
3. **Crafting Your Program Mission Statement:** A template to create your program rule of life to share with parents and your congregation.
4. **Mapping Out Your Choreography:** Meet with your clergy to clearly define expectations of all acolytes within the movements of your liturgy.
5. **Administrative Helps:** How to set up administrative support such as communication, scheduling, and debriefing.
6. **A Sample Acolyte Retreat:** An outline to help you schedule and gather youth for an acolyte lead retreat that concludes with your leads training younger acolytes in a general acolyte training.
7. **A Guided Eucharist:** A visual handout to discuss the liturgy and its movements at a retreat and/or training.
8. **A Visual Tour Guide:** A visual dictionary of artifacts and memorials found in your sacred space to use in training. Items are noted below each illustration. For training, acolytes may want to draw lines from the words to the illustrated object like a matching game.
9. **The Choreography of Processions:** A visual map to discuss the choreography of the four primary movements of liturgy to use in training.
10. **Church Manners for Acolytes:** A visual discussion tool to discuss manners and etiquette in training.
11. **Posters** (for hanging in your acolyte room, vesting space, or sacristy):
    Your Preworship Checklist
    Movements and Standards
    Censing and Bell Ringing
    The Holy Eucharist
12. **Debriefing Your Service:** Offering questions for reflection postliturgy.
13. **Commissioning Service**
14. **An Order of Worship Game**
15. **Acolyte Prayers**

The Ministry of the Acolyte

As a four-fold ministry of service to the Lord's altar:

1. We recognize that the altar is a focal point of our worship, representing the Body of Christ through which
   we receive communion. It is with utmost respect that we serve the Lord's altar.

2. Lead worship. As an acolyte, our place at the altar and presence in the sanctuary of the church puts us in a position of leadership second only to the clergy. Our presence must be absolutely respectful, humble, and fully present to the mystery that happens at each worship service.

3. Serve God's people. Our order is one of service to God and to our brothers and sisters. By our hands, worship moves through the liturgy, directing the people of God to the Holy Scripture, the altar, and each other as appropriate.

4. Model discipleship wherever we go, living into the best version of our commandment to "Love others as I have loved you" as given to us by Jesus.

Expectations

As part of your committed ministry to the Lord's altar, we expect you to:

1. Come prepared, wearing appropriate clothing: closed-toed shoes, respectful church attire. No gum, candy, or distracting accessories. Come rested, hydrated, and ready.

2. Arrive thirty minutes before the start of your service.

3. Be vested and have your instrument prepared fifteen minutes before the start of your service.

4. Fully participate in the entirety of the liturgy in which you are serving.

5. Be a calm, focused presence during worship. Follow your best rules of etiquette.

6. Be prepared to assist clergy and other ministers in any moment on the day you are scheduled to serve.

Crafting Your Way of Life

BEGIN BY CRAFTING A PURPOSE STATEMENT.

What is your current goal? What do you believe?

DECLARE YOUR BELIEFS.

What do you seek? What are three to five core concepts or foundational beliefs that you would like to keep in front of yourself at all times?

TOOLS

Define the skills, attributes, character strengths, experiences, and spiritual gifts that help you to be who you are.

SHORT-TERM GOALS

List your three to five short-term goals that are quintessential to your current happiness.

YOUR WAY OF LIFE

Who are you? What is your greatest strength? What is your greatest weakness? What disciplines do you chose to follow regularly?

ACCOUNTABILITY

Who will you share this with, if anyone? Can you name someone who will help you make this a reality?

Crafting Your Program Mission Statement

Program Title:

Program Mission:

Goals of the Ministry:

1. _____

2. _____

3. _____

Expectation of Acolytes:

Expectation of Leaders/Mentors:

Expectation of Parents:

Spiritual Growth and Development

1. _____

2. _____

3. _____

4. _____

5. _____

Organization of Ministry

• _____

• _____

• _____

• _____

• _____

Roles and Responsibilities:

Mapping Out Your Choreography

It is important to outline every step of the movements and drama of your church service. Each phase of the liturgy should be mapped out and taught using three techniques:

1. A handout for visual learners (see the samples we've included within this appendix.
2. A telling of the story for auditory learners.
3. A rehearsal for kinetic learners.

All three styles should be included in a training session to be effective. For those with high mass services involving many people and processions, each and every movement should be diagrammed so that there is no confusion of the expectations placed on acolytes, especially those who are assisting at the altar. Here are points to review with your clergy in advance of your training.

1. Discuss and design a seating chart for your space.
2. Address the four movements of the liturgy in which acolytes have responsibility:
    1. Entering procession
    2. Gospel procession
    3. Communion: setting and clearing the altar
    4. Exiting procession
    5. Special events such as Holy Baptism, the Rite of Confirmation, etc.
3. For each movement, define the following:
    1. What cue moves acolytes to their starting position?
    2. What cue begins the movement?
    3. What specific steps do each acolyte take in this movement? Diagrams are invaluable.
    4. How do acolytes return instruments to their places?
    5. When does the movement end for each specific acolyte?

Administrative Helps

Scheduling and communication can be the most complicated task for the acolyte leader. And much depends on your budget, size of program, and administrative assistance you may get from your church staff.

DIRECTORY/ROSTER

All of your contact information should be kept in one document or location. Include full name, address, e-mail and cell phone, date of birth, grade, school attending, and parents' or guardians' contact information.

No budget: A Word or Google document shared with all (or limited to a few).

Low budget: MinHub (*http://minhubapp.com*) or MinHub Youth enables you to track ministry data whether you have 5 or 500 youth. It allows you to collect contact information, photos, and sort individuals into groups as well as track conversations and attendance. It will also generate reports.

Moderate budget: Church Management Software from ACS (*https://www.acstechnologies.com*) or a similar integrated membership app allows your church to streamline all communication, databases, and scheduling in one system.

E-MAIL COMMUNICATION

Most churches now send e-newsletters over paper communications today. There are a variety of companies that offer these resources from basic free formats to expensive subscriptions with lots of bells and whistles. Following the Episcopal Church's *Model Policies for the Protection of Children and Youth*,[40] never contact children or youth without cc'ing a parent or guardian. Depending on your church's privacy policy, this information should not be readily accessible to others.

No budget: MailChimp (*https://mailchimp.com*).

Low budget: Constant Contact (*https://www.constantcontact.com*), Vertical Response (*https://www.verticalresponse.com*), and Emma (*https://myemma.com*) are the most popular and highly rated.

Moderate budget: Custom coded e-mail newsletters that can be created from other platforms such as ACS (noted above).

MOBILE COMMUNICATION

Leaving voicemail messages is becoming a thing of the past, and many families have dropped their landlines. Sending group texts is the way to go.

No budget: Create a group with everyone's cell-phone number and send texts.

Low budget: There is a variety of apps and social media. MinHub (noted above) can e-mail and text groups within your database.

Moderate budget: One Call Now (*http://www.onecallnow.com*) is a messaging service.

---

40. *https://www.forma.church/uploads/files/model-policy-for-the-protection-of-children-and-youth-2018_125.pdf* (accessed May 16, 2018).

SCHEDULING AND SIGN-UPS

In some ways, this can be the most time-consuming task. Families juggle multiple activities every day of the week.

No budget: Create a Google doc (*https://www.google.com/docs/about*) and have everyone log in to note when they are or aren't available. Or create a Doodle poll (*https://doodle.com*) listing dates and times for individuals to let you know if they are available, not available, or maybe available.

Low budget: SignUpGenius (*https://www.signupgenius.com*) is free, but an upgrade is helpful for multiple administrators. Participants choose which services or days they wish to serve. It sends automated reminder e-mails a day or two prior to the scheduled date.

Moderate budget: On MinistrySchedulerPro (*https://www.ministryschedulerpro.com*) participants mark out days they cannot serve, and the app will build a schedule for you. It sends out reminders and creates quarterly calendars.

SOCIAL MEDIA

Ask your acolytes what platform they would like to use to highlight their ministry. Create a plan and post regularly. Make sure it is integrated into your church's social media presence. Create specific groups for acolytes only if the momentum builds and bubbles up within them. Never create a social media platform and impress it upon them; organic growth is paramount.

DEBRIEFING

It is important to evaluate and tell the story of your experience. Debriefing questions can be posted and reviewed in vesting rooms. They can be included in a weekly e-mail to parents, or leads can text conversations to their teams to build feedback. Without a debrief process as part of your administration, you cannot grow and learn. See the form you can duplicate to use and share in this appendix entitled "Debriefing your service."

All debrief questions have the same general process to them:

1. What happened?
2. Why is that important? What can we learn from what happened?
3. What can we do to strengthen, change, or edit based on what happened?

John Dewey said, "We do not learn from experience. . . . We learn from reflecting on experience."

A Sample Acolyte Retreat⁴¹

PURPOSE

To produce a small group of "leads" (senior acolytes) that are empowered to train younger acolytes, participate fully (with ownership) in a worship service, and are able to manage teams of acolyte servers when scheduled.

- To establish norms for service, decorum, and respect at the altar.
- To update equipment and vestment uses: crosses, robes, care of the acolyte room, etc.
- To establish expectations of leads and frequency of service.
- To build a community based on a common understanding of serving God's altar as a ministry.

ADVANCE PREPARATION

- Communication to all involved.
- Gather food and preparation supplies.

SCHEDULE (WITHOUT OVERNIGHT)

Friday

6:00 p.m. **Arrival**
Cook as a community, following the jobs already assigned.

7:00 p.m. **Dinner**
Eat at single table, family style.

8:00 p.m. **Theology** (why we do what we do)
Offer experiential learning through games, such as the one found in this appendix. You can also download a power point *Jeopardy!* game for acolytes at *www.churchpublishing.org/iserveatgodsaltar.*

9:30 p.m. **Movie Break**
Show a movie about being called, such as *Whale Rider, Moana, Dead Poets Society,* or *Chariots of Fire.* Pass the popcorn!

11:00 p.m. **A Guided Eucharist**
Adjourn to the sanctuary. Create an experience of worship that is extraordinary using candles, incense, and music. Include all the actions acolytes assume: processions, candles, incense, lavabo, and altar setup step-by-step. Have them take on roles and follow along with the handout in this appendix.

---

41. This is an example of a retreat that Roger offers at Church of the Good Shepherd in Augusta, Georgia. Tweak the format to fit your needs and your acolytes.

11:45 p.m. Depart
Everyone leaves to go home for the night, to return in the morning.

Saturday

8:30 a.m. Morning Prayer (eat breakfast at home)

9:00 a.m. Etiquette
Practice the many roles of being an acolyte: How we carry our instruments. How we walk. Sitting still. Focusing practices. Standards and dress. Sizing and fitting of robes.

10:00 a.m. Choreography
Know when to move and how to move. Standard seating chart. Standing procession chart. (Provide pictures or diagrams of your church sanctuary.)

11:00 a.m. Commissioning Service for Leads

11:30 a.m. Lunch
Sandwiches for lunch, organized and cleaned up by leads.

12:00 p.m. Game Plan for Training
Review as necessary. Overflow hour for inevitable schedule needs and arrival of younger acolytes.

1:00 p.m. Acolyte Training
Leads lead rotations of thirty minutes each, round-robin style:

1. Holds and movements.
2. Choreography.
3. Review the service: what to do and when to do it.

Parents who are present build the upcoming schedules and rota of teams.

2:30 p.m. Clean Up
Leads clean up, set up for Sunday, and debrief.

3:00 p.m. Adjourn

A Guided Eucharist

The Holy Eucharist: Rite II

The Word of God

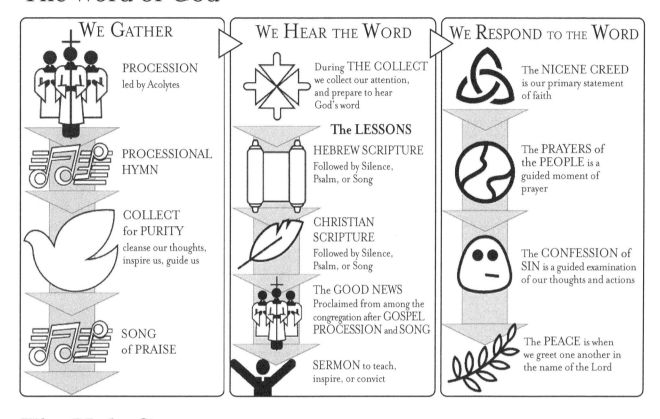

We Gather

PROCESSION
led by Acolytes

PROCESSIONAL
HYMN

COLLECT
for PURITY
cleanse our thoughts,
inspire us, guide us

SONG
of PRAISE

We Hear the Word

During THE COLLECT
we collect our attention,
and prepare to hear
God's word

The LESSONS
HEBREW SCRIPTURE
Followed by Silence,
Psalm, or Song

CHRISTIAN
SCRIPTURE
Followed by Silence,
Psalm, or Song

The GOOD NEWS
Proclaimed from among the
congregation after GOSPEL
PROCESSION and SONG

SERMON to teach,
inspire, or convict

We Respond to the Word

The NICENE CREED
is our primary statement
of faith

The PRAYERS of
the PEOPLE is a
guided moment of
prayer

The CONFESSION of
SIN is a guided examination
of our thoughts and actions

The PEACE is when
we greet one another in
the name of the Lord

The Holy Communion

The Great Thanksgiving

OFFERTORY
our treasure, our song,
and gifts of bread and wine
are offered to God

**THE GREAT
THANKSGIVING**

A CALL
to ACTION

Our JOY expressed
in WORD and SONG

We KNEEL in reverence

We Remember the Story

God CREATES,
humanity SINS,
God JUDGES
Christ REDEEMS

The story of the
FIRST
COMMUNION

The MYSTERY of
FAITH proclaimed

Sanctified GIFTS
Sanctified PEOPLE

We Receive the Sacrament

The LORD'S PRAYER
is our model for personal
prayer, and prepares us to
receive communion

The BREAKING of the
BREAD is the moment
in which Jesus dies

HOLY COMMUNION
is presented

We are SENT with a
BLESSING, PROCESSING
with song in the world

The Holy Eucharist: Rite II

A Visual Tour Guide

THE COMPONENTS OF A CHURCH BUILDING

In the earliest days of the church (100 CE), people worshiped in homes and in secret because public displays of Christian worship were outlawed in the Roman Empire. Eventually, Christians were permitted to build new spaces for worship and the Church evolved to meet the ever-changing needs of the culture. Your church building most likely reflects one of the following architectural styles.

0–300 CE
Most church communities worshiped in houses, secret rooms, or caves.

300–1100 CE
As the Roman Empire fell into decline and the Church split into Western and Eastern traditions, the basilica with its centralized domes became home to Christians.

1000–1200 CE
Romanesque churches grew taller with the development of buttressing technology. Most took on a cruciform layout and were made of stone.

1100–1300 CE
At the height of the Middle Ages, flying buttress technology was used to create the "skyscrapers of the Middle Ages." Gothic cathedrals are known for their intricate construction and decoration.

1400–1700 CE
Baroque churches are the product of the Renaissance architects. Their elaborate style came to the Americas with Spanish and French missionaries.

1700–1900 CE
The colonial churches of early American expansion were simple, cost effective, and smaller than their ancestors.

CHURCHES TODAY

Modern churches may emulate one of the historical styles above or they may be completely different. There are common components to most churches that may give you some idea of where people are asking you to go and in which section of the structure various parts of the liturgy takes place.

From the Latin, *sanctus* meaning "holy," the **sanctuary** is the entire worship space of a church. Some people refer to the specific section of the church building that houses the altar as the sanctuary. The **narthex**, from the Greek meaning "giant funnel," is an antechamber (entrance) where those who were not permitted to worship with the congregation could still witness the service. The **nave** (Latin *navis*, meaning "ship") is the central area of the church, where you will find pews or chairs for the worshiping congregation. For many churches, if you look up to the ceiling, it will look like the hull of a ship. Any space between the rows of seats is called an **aisle**, from the Latin meaning "wing." Walking down the center aisle, you will arrive at the **crossing**, the intersection of the central aisle

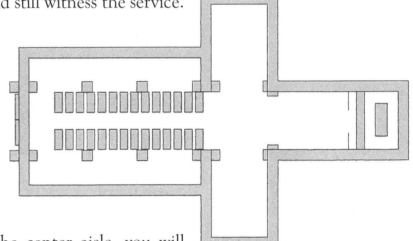

and the transept aisles. The **transept** (Latin *transeptum* meaning "across") gives the footprint of the church a cruciform shape; either of two parts of the transept form the arms of a cross. "Crossing" the crossing, you will enter the **choir** area. Sometimes this is separated from the nave by steps, a rood screen, or altar rail. From the Latin *chorus*, meaning "a dance in a circle," the choir is a section of the church that lies between the nave and the **chancel**. Again, this name comes from a Latin word, *cancelli*, meaning "crossbars." It is here that you will find the altar, credence table, and often stands for crosses, torches, and banners. In some churches the (singing) choir sits in this area on one side or both, or they may sit behind the altar or in the balcony which hovers above the narthex looking down into the sanctuary.

Every worship space is different. Below you can see some other possible locations that may or may not exist in your church. Take a walk through your space and identify if any of the elements shown above or below are part of your experience. Draw the footprint of your own sanctuary and label its areas.

Some churches have a **cloister**, a covered walkway between buildings or surrounding an atrium. An **atrium** is a large, open air or sky-lit space surrounded by a building. The **vestibule** is a passage or room between the doors to the outside and the narthex. Processions typically "line up" in the narthex or vestibule before a service. The **portal** is a doorway or collection of doorways that lead from the narthex to the nave. Many churches have one or more **chapels** as part of their sanctuary, often set to the side. From the Latin *cappa*, meaning "cape," this is a place of prayer or worship attached to a larger worship space. In some churches there is an **altar of repose** where the consecrated bread and wine for Holy Communion rests in an aumbry or tabernacle if not kept near the main altar in the chancel. If there is a Holy Communion on Good Friday, this is where the elements are kept. Most churches also have a baptismal font at the entrance or side area of the sanctuary, called the **baptistry**. From the Greek, *baptizein* meaning "immerse, dip in water," this is an intentionally designed space.

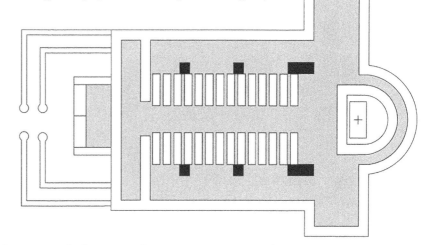

From the outside, a Gothic church is easy to recognize. The **dome** (Greek *doma*, meaning "housetop") is a spherical vault that forms the roof of the structure. The **clerestory** is the upper section of the wall that is often filled with stained glass windows; it is supported by **buttressing**, the stonework designed to support the walls, allowing them to be built higher without interior support. The **undercroft**, sometimes known as the crypt, is the lower level of a church.

The **altar rail** with **kneelers** surrounding the chancel area in Grace Episcopal Church in Traverse City, Michigan. The free-standing wooden **altar** is flanked by **torches** and two chairs for the presider and an assistant. A **lectern** is on the left while seating for others such as acolytes and ministers of communion are on the right. Looking closely, you can also see **processional crosses**, the **credence table**, the **sanctuary lamp,** and an **altar cross** flanked by vases of flowers on the retable.

The altar at St. Matthew's Episcopal Church in Wilton, Connecticut, is covered with an **altar frontal** with palms scattered in front for Palm Sunday. To the left of the altar is the **lectern**, flanked by **torches**. The **aumbry** is located on the left wall behind the lectern. Behind the altar are the **organ** and its **pipes** and seating for the choir.

The free-standing **altar** at St. Matthew's Episcopal Church in Wheeling, West Virginia, is covered with a **frontal**. It has a **Missal** on a stand, a **veiled chalice**, and **eucharistic candles** on it. To the left is a **credence table** and **lectern** while the **pulpit** is located on the right. **Prayer desks** (a kneeler with a small lectern) and chairs for the officiants are located on both the right and left of the altar, with the **bishop's cathedra** (chair or throne) behind the **rood screen** (a richly carved wooden, metal, or stone screen that separates the nave from the chancel) on the left. An **altar rail** and **kneelers** provides the divider between the chancel and the nave, where the **pews** are located. Behind the rood screen you can glimpse the organ on the right with **pews** for the choir to sit on both sides. The **altar cross** sits on the **fixed altar** on the far east wall, in front of the reredos.

Reredos, retable, or dossal? A **reredos** generally begins from the floor behind an altar and covers the majority of the east wall, while a **retable** begins from the altar itself and can be freestanding or attached to the wall. **Dossals** are simple fabric hangings or a created piece of artwork that stands behind the altar, also against the east wall. Reredos became popular in the early renaissance as the church commissioned artists to create beautiful spaces inside sanctuaries. They fell out of fashion and did not return to the church until the classical period of the eighteenth century. The retable may hold flowers and candlesticks. This image is of the reredos at Washington National Cathedral in Washington, DC, where the annual National Acolyte Festival is held in October.

VESTMENTS

Vestments are the clothing that those who serve at God's altar wear. Each church has its own tradition and practice as to who wears what; do you know what the names of your vestments are?

Bishops

The ministry of a bishop is to represent Christ and the Church, particularly as apostle, chief priest, and pastor of a diocese; to guard the faith, unity, and discipline of the whole Church; to proclaim the Word of God; to act in Christ's name for the reconciliation of the world and building up of the Church; and to ordain others to continue in Christ's ministry. Acolytes are often called upon to serve as a bishop's chaplain when a bishop makes a parish visitation.

A bishop wears a **stole**—a long, narrow, often decorated piece of fabric worn around the neck to signify an ordained person. It is like putting on the "yoke of Christ." Bishops wear the stole over both shoulders. They also wear an **Episcopal ring**, a sign of their office as a bishop. It is worn on the third finger of the right hand and is often engraved with a signet or the diocesan seal. It used to be used to seal (with wax) important documents. The **chimere** (a loose robe, typically red) worn by a bishop was adapted from a riding cloak of colonial days. The **cope**, an intricate cape, was historically worn to keep warm. A bishop perhaps is most recognized by the **mitre** (headwear) and **crozier** (staff resembling a shepherd's crook) that symbolize their authority and pastoral office.

The presiding bishop (currently The Most Reverend Michael Bruce Curry) is the chief pastor and primate of the Episcopal Church. A primate is the most senior bishop of one of the thirty-nine provinces of the Anglican Communion, of which the Episcopal Church is part. The **primatial staff** (crozier) is a symbol of the authority of the presiding bishop. All bishops are elected by the people (lay and ordained representatives) of their diocese in a democratic process. The presiding bishop is elected to serve a term of nine years by the House of Bishops at General Convention.

Priests

The ministry of a priest is to represent Christ and the Church, particularly as pastor to the people; to share in the overseeing of the Church with their bishop; to proclaim the gospel; to administer the sacraments; and to bless and declare pardon in the name of God. Priests wear a variety of vestments; those most universal about all ordained people is a **clerical collar**, a stiff white band that closes at the back of the neck, and a **stole** (often the color of the church season) worn over both shoulders. A priest may also wear a **cassock** and **surplice** (a plain garment that buttons down the center and extends to the ankles with a white garment with long sleeves on top) or an **alb**, a white linen tunic that extends to the ankles and is worn with a rope **cincture** tied at the waist. At celebrations, the celebrant at the Eucharist may also wear a **cope** (cape) that is fastened at the front with a clasp, called a **morse**. Some priests also wear a **biretta**, a square cap with three flat projections and a pom-pom on top. The outermost garment that a priest wears when celebrating the Holy Eucharist is a **chasuble**, usually the same color as their stole according to the church season.

Deacons

The ministry of a deacon is to represent Christ and the Church, particularly as a servant of those in need; and to assist bishops and priests in the proclamation of the gospel and administration of the sacraments. Not all congregations are blessed to have a deacon, but when one is present, they typically read the Gospel and set up (and clean up) the altar for Holy Communion. They also wear a clerical collar and a **stole**; the stole is draped over the left shoulder.

Acolytes

Acolytes serve alongside bishops, priests, and deacons at God's altar in many capacities. They typically wear an **alb** (a white linen tunic that extends to the ankles) with or without a **cincture**. They may also wear a **cassock** (a plain lightweight garment that extends to the ankles that is typically black or red. It can have buttons down the center or be double-breasted. Over the cassock is usually a **scapular** (a white covering with no sleeves that extends to the ankles) or a **cotta** (like a surplice, but shorter and with shorter sleeves or no sleeves at all).

MOVEMENTS AND ACTIONS

Walking

When walking, especially if you are carrying any object, take short steps. Concentrate on stepping heel to toe. Imagine that there is a string tied to the back of your head; pull on it to improve your posture. And don't forget—glide, do not lumber.

Bowing

Bowing is a sign of reverence and honor. You should do a simple bow (lowering of your head at the neck) when you hear Jesus's name, <u>any time</u> you pass the altar with empty hands, in the Nicene Creed when the words "he became incarnate from the Virgin Mary" are said, and before and after approaching the altar for communion or at any other time. A profound bow is usually used (bending at the waist to look at your feet) when others are kneeling and you are standing (such as during the confession or eucharistic prayer.) Always watch to see when the priest bows, then follow along. Never bow when carrying a cross, candle, book, etc.

Standing and Sitting

When standing, keep your feet shoulder width apart. Practice not swaying. When not holding onto anything, fold your hands palm to palm at your waist or breast with your elbows touching the side of your body. When holding something with one hand, hold the other, palm in, to your solar plexus. In most cases, when holding something always use two hands. Your default position should always be to stand. Only sit or kneel when the celebrant does—keep a watchful eye on what they do! When sitting, do not cross your knees or ankles. Lay your hands on your knees and sit straight (do not lounge). Do not twirl or play with your cincture, cross, or robes. Remember—the congregation can see everything that you do!

Candle Lighting

Lighting and extinguishing candles can be easy or quite difficult, depending on how many candles are in your chancel area. Facing the altar, think about the two sides of the altar—the left side has been known as the "gospel side" and the right as the "epistle side." A well-known mantra is that the gospel cannot be proclaimed without the people, so the gospel side candle/s do not burn alone. An epistle is a letter, such as the letters the apostle Paul wrote to the early churches around the Mediterranean Sea.

God's love and light radiates from the empty cross. Always light the epistle side candles first, then the gospel side candles. Reverse the order when extinguishing them, gospel side out first followed by epistle side. Light candles closest to the cross first, moving outward. Follow the arrows and numbered order below for lighting (white circles) and extinguishing (dark circles).

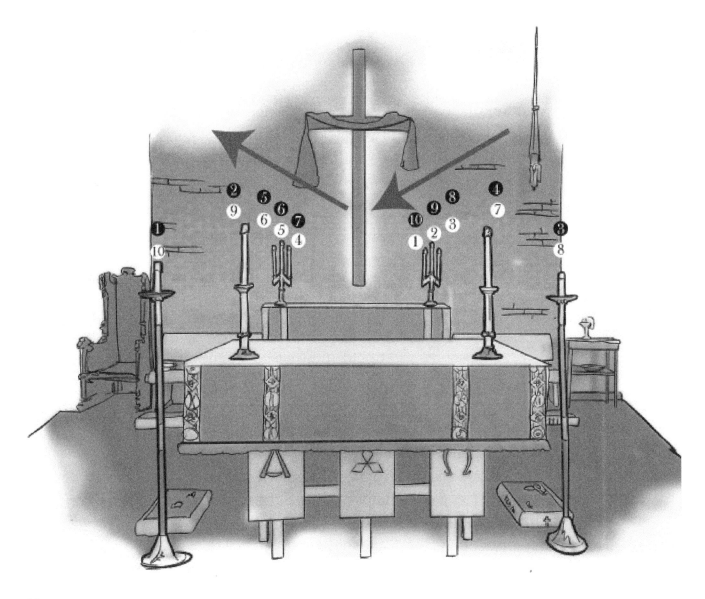

Making a Sign of the Cross

Make the sign of the cross with your right hand, touching your fingers first to your forehead (Father), heart (Son), left shoulder (Holy), right shoulder (Spirit), then clasp your hands in front of you. You can make the sign of the cross:

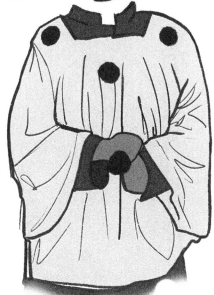

- During the Gloria in Excelsis at the words: "Jesus Christ, with the Holy Spirit, in the glory of God the Father. Amen."
- During the Gospel reading at the words: "The Holy Gospel of our Lord Jesus Christ according to . . ."
- During the Nicene Creed at the words: "We look for the resurrection of the dead, and the life of the world to come. Amen."
- During the absolution following the confession at: "Almighty God have mercy on you . . ."
- At the conclusion of the eucharistic prayer at the words: "The Gifts of God for the People of God."
- At the blessing: "And the blessing of God Almighty, the Father, the Son, and the Holy Spirit be amongst you and remain with you always."

SACRED OBJECTS AND WHERE TO FIND THEM

There are numerous sacred objects used in our liturgies, and acolytes are often tasked with bringing them from place to place. Of most importance are the elements: the bread, wine, oil, and water that symbolize our sacraments of Holy Eucharist and Holy Baptism. Water is the element by which we enter into Christ's body through baptism. Oil is the element by which we are blessed and sealed as Christ's own forever at baptism or when anointed for healing. Bread is the element we eat in remembrance of Jesus Christ. Wine is the element we drink to remember the new covenant we have in Jesus Christ.

You will find the following items on the altar (perhaps not all at the same time) during the Holy Eucharist: The **Missal** (or service or altar book) contains all the liturgical rites and prayers necessary for celebrating Holy Communion. It rests on a **missal stand** or pillow to help guide the priest in leading the liturgy. The **tabernacle** holds consecrated elements. The **Gospel Book** is a decorative book (sometimes red, sometimes covered in a gold case) that

contains only the Gospel readings from the lectionary. It is typically processed to be read from in the midst of the congregation by the Gospeller, who is either a priest or deacon. A crucifer and torches typically lead the procession with the torches flanking the book as the Gospel is proclaimed. The altar frontal is a parament, usually decorated and matching the color of the season of the church year. It covers the surface of the altar and drapes to face the congregation. The altar frontal is covered with a **fair linen**, which is typically embroidered with five crosses. It offers a protective layer upon which the sacred vessels will be placed. In preparation for the Eucharist, an empty chalice is placed on the altar. On top of the **chalice** is "stacked" a **purificator**, a **paten** (often with a large host on it), a **pall**, and maybe a **burse**. Some congregations place a **veil** (in the season's color) on top of all of this. **Eucharistic candles** and an **altar cross** are in a prominent position also. This is the altar at Church of the Good Shepherd in Augusta, Georgia.

Before Holy Communion, the gifts of the people of God are brought forth to the altar at the offertory. There is often a table that holds all of these items in the back of the nave for ushers and oblation bearers to bring them forth during the singing of a hymn (often the doxology). The **alms basins** (or offertory plates) can be made of metal, glass, or a basket to gather and present the offering of the congregation of financial gifts as well as gifts from the field: bread and wine. A large ornamental jug called a **ewer** is used for carrying larger quantities of wine. For less wine, glass cruets or metal flagons are used. The **bread box** carries unconsecrated bread that is brought to the altar at the offertory also; it is a small ornamental box made of wood, stone, or metal. A **ciborium** might be used in its stead—a large chalice-shaped container with a lid made of metal.

The Credence Table

The **credence table** is a side table in the chancel area of a church. It is use to hold the elements and vessels necessary for the rite of Holy Communion. Credence means "the likelihood of something being true or believable." This table is home to the items that become the Body and Blood of Jesus Christ, lending the Holy Communion "credence." Some credence tables are attached to the east wall of the sanctuary while others are freestanding.

Acolytes often bring these items back and forth from this table to the altar to assist the celebrant. You will find a **chalice** (a cup with a foot, used for drinking) covered with a **purificator** (a linen cloth used to wipe, or purify, the chalice after someone drinks from it; a **bread box** that contains wafers or unconsecrated bread); a **lavabo bowl** and **lavabo towel** (for washing and drying the priest's hands before the beginning of the Great Thanksgiving); and a large **paten**. Sometimes the **Missal** and **missal stand** will be on this table for an acolyte to bring to the altar when it is being set. Extra cruets of wine or water may also rest, plus extra chalices and purificators. This particular credence table does not have bread or wine on it, as they have yet to be brought to the altar during the offertory portion of the service.

"The Stack"

Locally sometimes called the "stack" or the "veiled chalice," the altar guild will prepare for Holy Communion by "dressing" the chalice with the many items that will be used for setting the altar. This may be found on the credence table or already on the altar at the beginning of the service. Starting from the inside or bottom, you find the **chalice**, which has a **purificator** draped over it, with a **paten** on top (with a **priest's host**—the bread or wafer used in the eucharistic prayer and broken at the Fraction—in it). The celebrant (or

deacon if they are preparing the altar) will pour wine and a small amount of water into the chalice. The paten is a plate typically made of metal, used for holding bread during the administration of Holy Communion. The chalice **pall**, a stiff square cover, is placed over the paten. It may be later used to place upon the chalice filled with wine to keep flying insects out. The **corporal** is folded on top; this is a square white cloth that is unfolded and spread on the altar before the chalice and paten is placed upon it. Its purpose is to collect any crumbs from the Eucharist that might fall during the prayer of consecration. On top of this might be a **burse**, which is like a fabric pocket for holding extra purificators. Some congregations continue to cover this whole "stack" with a chalice **veil**, a liturgical vestment that was probably developed in the Middle Ages to protect the chalice while being carried to the altar from the credence table or other area. It is appropriately colored for the church season.

Incense

This thurifer wears an **alb** while swinging a **thurible** filled with smoking incense. Incense is material consisting of biological matter (bark, oil, plant matter, charcoal, etc.) that produces a fragrant smoke when burned. **Tongs** are used to move the incense from the **boat** to the thurible. The smoke that rises and permeates the sanctuary represents our prayers as they ascend to heaven. Not all churches use incense—you can usually tell which churches do because when you enter their sanctuary you can smell its presence that permeates the air long after worship is over.

The Aumbry

The doors of this **aumbry** are open. When this structure is on the altar, it is called a tabernacle. Within this aumbry you find consecrated bread in a **bread box**, a **cruet** of consecrated wine, and gluten-free wafers covered by a **purificator** inside. A **sanctuary lamp** remains lit at all times consecrated elements are in the aumbry.

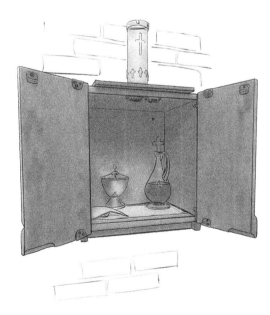

Holy Baptism

When Holy Baptism is part of the liturgy of the Holy Eucharist, it follows the sermon. Godparents and parents (plus the candidates to be baptized if they are old enough) make promises to reject evil, turn, and follow Jesus Christ. Following vows and prayers, water from the **baptismal font** is poured upon the candidate's head in the name of the Father, the Son, and the Holy Spirit. They are then marked with oil as Christ's own forever with oil (chrism) on their forehead. The **pascal candle** is lit at every baptism, funeral, and throughout the fifty days of the Easter season, celebrating the resurrection.

Candles

An acolyte wearing a **cassock** and **scapular** lighting the **Advent wreath** for the second Sunday of Advent, a time of preparing for the birth of Christ.

The Choreography of Processions

ENTERING AND EXITING PROCESSIONS

Thurifer _____

Boat Bearer _____

Verger _____

First Crucifer _____

First Torchbearers _____

[Seasonal Banner Bearer] _____

Choir _____

[Second Crucifer] _____

[Second Torchbearers] _____

[Church Banner Bearer] _____

Gospel Bearer _____

Eucharistic Ministers _____

Deacon _____

Assisting Clergy _____

Preacher _____

Celebrant_____

THE GOSPEL PROCESSION

Verger _____

First Crucifer _____

First Torchbearers _____

Gospel Bearer _____

Gospel Reader/Deacon _____

Thurifer _____

Boat Bearer _____

THE OFFERTORY PROCESSION

Thurifer _____

Boat Bearer _____

Verger _____

Second Crucifer _____

Second Torchbearers _____

Ushers _____

Oblation Bearers _____

Church Manners for Acolytes

THOU SHALT . . .

Say Hello

- Smile, be friendly! Introduce yourself to someone you don't know if appropriately timed.

- You are sometimes the first person that people see at church, and you should represent your community as best you can, welcoming all to worship.

Arrive Early

- You should be present and vested fifteen minutes before your scheduled service.

- If you are late, please call or text the lead or acolyte mentor/master.

Be Respectful in the Sanctuary

- The worship space is not "normal space." It is set apart, and consecrated. Please treat it that way.

- Lower your voice when speaking, and never talk during the service.

Dress for Reverence

- How one dresses is also a sign of respect, which is one reason acolytes wear robes. But think about what goes under them as well as what will show.

- Carrying objects and walking up and down stairs need sturdy shoes.

- Be aware of the temperature and that you'll be wearing extra layers of covering.

- Spend a moment on your appearance before coming to church.

- Do not wear acolyte robes that have stains, wax, or tears, damages. Set them aside for repair and washing.

- Return and hang all vestments to their appropriate labeled location.

Sit Well

- Feet should be flat on the floor.
- Bum should be either all the way to the back of the chair, or on the front edge, to force the back to straighten.
- Hold your head high. Do not slouch.

Yawn Courteously (If Necessary)

- In the moment of a yawn, quickly cover your mouth with hand, back of hand, or forearm.
- If you have drawn attention by the yawn, excuse yourself, "Sorry, that just came over me suddenly."
- Get a good night's sleep the night before!

Pay Attention

- Fully participate in the worship service. This includes standing, kneeling, and sitting at appropriate times.
- Sing, recite prayers, cross yourself when the Trinity is invoked (if that is your church's custom), and be aware of the other people in the chancel with you.

Bow

- When you walk in front of the altar, stopping to face it first in the middle. (See above.)
- When *receiving* or *giving* a holy vessel or instrument (such as a cruet, ewer, chalice, thurible, boat, alms basins, etc.).
- But not when you are holding something.

Make the Sign of the Cross

Sign the shape of the cross (head, heart, shoulder-shoulder, heart) anytime

- The Holy Trinity is invoked (Father, Son, Holy Spirit).
- You feel particularly moved to do so.
- Honoring the dead.
- You hear the sirens of first responders.

Maintaining Focus and Respect

The average human has an eight-second attention span, and that number is shrinking due to digital connectedness, according to a Microsoft study.[42] Focus is a muscle. Without work and exercise, it atrophies. The following tools will help you discipline yourself and give you guidance to pass along during your trainings.

Prepare

Before the service begins, spend a minute or two to breathe, calm, and quiet yourself. Close your eyes, find a quiet space, and just breathe for a moment. If you have trouble fidgeting, bring a worry stone or object in your pocket to discreetly bring comfort and anxiety relief.

Understand

You cannot lead a worship service you do not understand. Come to acolyte training, read the worship program, follow along in the prayer book. Your focus must be securely on the liturgy, not on anything anywhere, or anyone else.

Unplug

Turn your phone off twenty to thirty minutes before worship. Leave it off during worship. (This may be the most difficult thing of all! Perhaps phones can be placed in a basket in the sacristy for all worship leaders.)

Eat and Drink

Make sure you have appropriate food and hydration before coming to serve. Orange juice or coffee can help.

Fidgeting

If, during the service, you cannot sit completely still, put something in your hands. Hold the prayer book or hymnal, bring a fidget stone or hand cross. Do not allow yourself to bounce knees and twirl crosses or cinctures.

Breathe

Anytime you feel your focus waning, or you catch yourself daydreaming, take in a big deep breath. The air will reset you, wake you up, and bring you back to the moment.

---

42. Kevin McSpadden, "You Now Have a Shorter Attention Span Than a Goldfish," *Time*, May 14, 2015, *http://time.com/3858309/attention-spans-goldfish/*, accessed July 23, 2018.

Your Preworship Checklist

30 MINUTES BEFORE WORSHIP: Turn off your phone.
Detox yourself from technology.

20 MINUTES BEFORE WORSHIP: Arrive at church, having eaten breakfast.
Use the restroom: toss the gum, straighten your clothes and hair.

15 MINUTES BEFORE WORSHIP: Vest.

Say hello. Smile, be friendly! You may be the first person people see at church, and you should welcome all to worship. Stay after worship to greet people before they go home.

Dress reverently. Never wear flip-flops. What you wear from the knees down is vital to your image as an acolyte. Be aware of the temperature and that your robes will add extra layers. Spend a moment checking on your appearance. Do not wear robes if they are stained with wine or wax or are damaged in any way. Set them aside for repair and washing. Return all vestments to their appropriate labeled location.

An alb fits if its shoulders are within one to two inches of your shoulder and its length falls below your knees.

A cotta fits if its sleeves are below your elbows and its length falls below your hips and above your knees.

Remember that the sanctuary is not "normal space." It is set apart and consecrated to God. Please treat it that way by lowering your voice when speaking. Never talk during the service.

10 MINUTES BEFORE WORSHIP: Check the candles; light if not already lit.
If you are a lead, assign roles, placements in procession, and seating arrangements.
If you are not a lead, check in and gather your implement (cross, candle, etc.)

5 MINUTES BEFORE WORSHIP: Gather with the other altar ministers. Pray.

Gracious God, the epitome of light and love: You call us to light the way for your people in a world of change and uncertainty. Grant to your acolytes reverent heartbeats, steady hands, and the will to persevere in service at your altar and at prayer. Bless and guide us by your wisdom and help us to spread your word throughout the world. Through Jesus Christ our Lord, who lives and reigns with you and the Holy Spirit, one God, now and forever. Amen.

Movements and Standards

PROCESSION ORDER

(left to right): Top: bishop, eucharistic ministers, banner bearer, crucifer, verger Bottom: celebrant, assisting clergy, deacon, book bearer, choir, seasonal banner, torchbearer, thruifer, boat bearer

HOLDING OBJECTS

- Stand straight.
- Use two hands.
- Keep the right distance behind whoever is in front of you.
- Mirror the person who is beside you.
- Bend elbows according to what you are holding.

WALKING

- Take short steps.
- Concentrate your step—heel to toe
- Imagine a string tied to the back of your head. Pull it to improve your posture.
- Glide, do not lumber.

STANDING

- Keep your feet a shoulder width apart.
- Practice not swaying.
- When not holding anything, fold hands palm to palm before your chest, elbows touching the side of your body.
- When holding something with one hand, hold the other palm in to your solar plexus.
- The default pose is to stand. Only sit or kneel when the celebrant does.

SITTING

- Sit up straight; do not lounge.
- Do not cross knees.
- Do not cross ankles.
- Lay hands flat on knees.
- Do not twirl or in any way play with your cincture or cross.

PREPARATION OF THE ALTAR

Preparing the altar is like getting ready for dinner, going back and forth from the kitchen to the dining room. In our case, it is moving back and forth from the credence table to the altar:

1. If the elements (bread and wine) are not brought to the altar from the congregation, get them from the credence table.
2. Give the chalice (stacked) to the celebrant or deacon at the altar.
3. Pass the bread box to the celebrant or deacon.
4. Pass the wine and water with the handles facing them.
5. Put away whatever they hand back to you.

Passing the cruets of wine and water:

1. Offer the wine cruet with your right hand.
2. Place the water cruet from your left hand to your right hand.
3. Receive the wine cruet with your left hand.
6. Offer the water cruet with your right hand.
7. Place the wine cruet from your left hand to your right hand.
8. Receive the water cruet with your left hand.
9. Return cruets to the credence table.

THE LAVABO

When offering the lavabo to wash the celebrant's hands:

1. Place the lavabo towel over your nondominant arm.
2. Place the lavabo bowl into your nondominant palm.
3. Hold the water cruet (by the handle) in your dominant hand.
4. Gently pour water over the celebrant's hands or fingers.
5. Offer your arm with the lavabo towel to the celebrant.
6. When they replace the towel, bow, and return all objects to the credence table.

Censing and Bell Ringing

CARRYING THE THURIBLE AND BOAT

1. Always carry the thurible in your right hand.
2. Always carry the boat in your left hand.
3. Swing the censer at full length during processions. Otherwise carry it by the chains just above the bowl.
4. If not carrying the boat, rest your left hand on your chest.

WHEN PASSING THE CENSER

1. Use your right hand to grasp the chains near the bowl.
2. Hold the disc with your left hand.
3. Pass the disc first, then offer the chains to the receiver.

CENSING PEOPLE (OR OBJECTS)

1. Bow to the people (or person or object).
2. Swing censer three times: center, left, right.
3. Bow again.

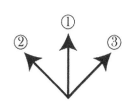

ORDER AND PROCESS FOR CENSING THE ALTAR PARTY

1. Bishop—three swings
2. Celebrant—three swings; two swings if a bishop is present
3. Assisting ministers—two swings

THE SANCTUS BELL is a small hand bell with a single tongue. Chiming bells are not forbidden but are not correct.

- Ring three strokes at the Sanctus (Holy, holy, holy).
- Ring one stroke just before the consecration begins.
- Ring three strokes when priest genuflects.
- Ring three strokes when the host is elevated.
- Ring three stokes when priest genuflects a second time.
- Ring one stroke when the celebrant receives communion.

The Holy Eucharist

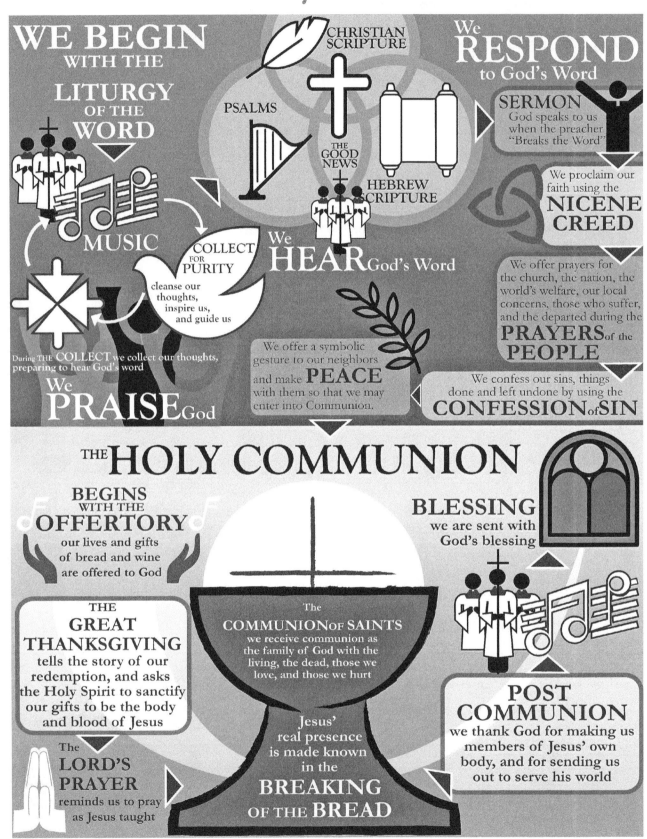

WE BEGIN WITH THE **LITURGY** OF THE **WORD**

MUSIC

COLLECT FOR PURITY — cleanse our thoughts, inspire us, and guide us

During THE COLLECT we collect our thoughts, preparing to hear God's word

We PRAISE God

CHRISTIAN SCRIPTURE

PSALMS

THE GOOD NEWS

HEBREW SCRIPTURE

We HEAR God's Word

We offer a symbolic gesture to our neighbors and make **PEACE** with them so that we may enter into Communion.

We RESPOND to God's Word

SERMON — God speaks to us when the preacher "Breaks the Word"

We proclaim our faith using the **NICENE CREED**

We offer prayers for the church, the nation, the world's welfare, our local concerns, those who suffer, and the departed during the **PRAYERS** of the **PEOPLE**

We confess our sins, things done and left undone by using the **CONFESSION** of **SIN**

THE **HOLY COMMUNION**

BEGINS WITH THE **OFFERTORY** — our lives and gifts of bread and wine are offered to God

THE **GREAT THANKSGIVING** tells the story of our redemption, and asks the Holy Spirit to sanctify our gifts to be the body and blood of Jesus

The **LORD'S PRAYER** reminds us to pray as Jesus taught

The **COMMUNION** of **SAINTS** we receive communion as the family of God with the living, the dead, those we love, and those we hurt

Jesus' real presence is made known in the **BREAKING** OF THE **BREAD**

BLESSING we are sent with God's blessing

POST COMMUNION we thank God for making us members of Jesus' own body, and for sending us out to serve his world

Debriefing Your Service

1. What was the message of today's worship?

2. In what ways did we fulfill or fall short of our duty in service at God's altar?

3. What should we start, stop, or continue doing?

4. Describe your experience of God today.

Commissioning Service[1]

The Examination

Celebrant: Friends in Christ Jesus, we are all baptized by the one Spirit into one Body, and given gifts for a variety of ministries for the common good. Our purpose is to commission these persons in the Name of God and of this congregation to the special ministry to which they are called, the ministry of acolyte.

The Celebrant asks the sponsors: Are these persons who stand before us prepared by a commitment to Christ as Lord, by regular attendance at worship, and by the knowledge of their duties, to exercise their ministry as an acolyte to the honor of God and the well-being of God's Church?

Sponsor: I believe they are.

Celebrant: You have been called to the acolyte ministry in this congregation. Will you, as long as you are engaged in this work, perform it with diligence?

Acolyte candidates: I will.

Celebrant: Will you faithfully and reverently execute the duties of your ministry to the honor of God, and the benefit of the members of this congregation?

Acolyte candidates: I will.

The Commissioning

Sponsor: I present to you these persons to be admitted to the ministry of acolyte in this congregation.

Celebrant: Do not be negligent, for the Lord has chosen you to stand God's presence, to minister to Christ, and to be Christ's minister.

Acolyte candidates: I will go to the altar of God.

Congregation: To the God of my joy and gladness.

Celebrant: Let us pray. (*Silence.*) O God: Bless the acolytes of your Church that they may so serve before your earthly altar in reverence and holiness, that they may attain, with your saints and angels, the joy of serving you and worshiping before your Heavenly Altar, through Jesus Christ our Lord. *Amen.*

In the Name of God and of this congregation, I commission you *N.* as an acolyte in this *Parish*, and give you this cross as a token of your ministry.

---

1. *The Book of Occasional Services 2003* (New York: Church Pension Fund, 2004), 183–84.

An Order of Worship Game

This is a helpful tool (and can be played as a timed game) for learning the order of worship. Duplicate the following pages (one per team or acolyte) and cut the words or phrases into slips, putting each set into an envelope. Provide your church's worship bulletin as a pattern to follow if desired. This works best with everyone sitting on the floor, sorting each item, and putting them all in order from beginning to end. Remove those words or phrases that are not part of your worship service depending on the season or special event, such as the confession of sin, which is not said during the Easter season. Insert other pieces (like baptism) when they occur. Once everyone has assembled their order of worship, review each portion of the liturgy and talk about what roles are played by acolytes during them. You can also insert those roles within the list of movements.

The Order of Worship

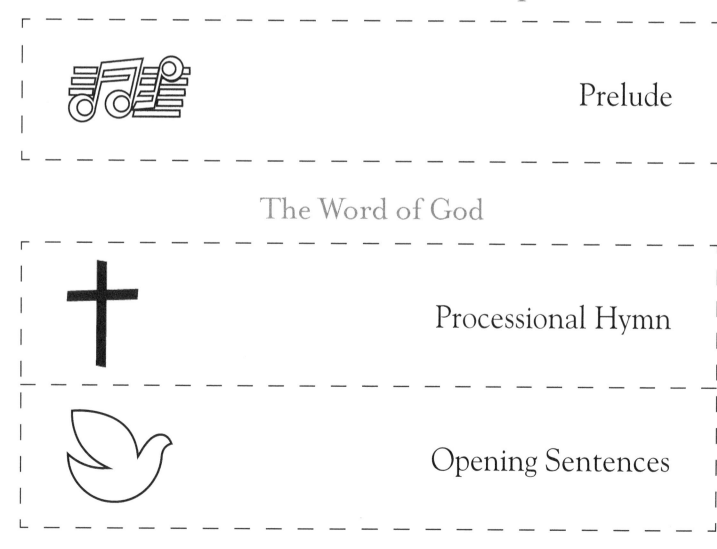

Prelude

The Word of God

Processional Hymn

Opening Sentences

 Song of Praise

 Collect of the Day

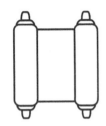 Old Testament Reading

 Psalm

 New Testament Reading

 Sequence (Gradual) Hymn

 Gospel Reading

 The Sermon

 [Holy Baptism]

 The Nicene Creed

 The Prayers of the People

 Confession of Sin

 Absolution of Sin

 The Peace

The Holy Communion

 The Offertory

 The Great Thanksgiving

 God's Redemption

 The Last Supper

 The Mystery of Faith

 Sanctification

 The Lord's Prayer

 The Breaking of the Bread (Fraction)

 Postcommunion Prayer

 Blessing

 Recessional Hymn

 Dismissal

 Postlude

Acolyte Actions

Light candles

Move the Gospel Book

Move the Missal (altar book)

Cense the altar

Set the altar

Collect the offering

Lavabo / washing of hands

Ring Sanctus bells

Assist with ablutions

Extinguish candles

Acolyte Prayers

A PRAYER FOR ACOLYTES

Almighty and everlasting God, who gives grace to those who minister; give your blessing, we pray, upon your acolytes appointed to serve you before your altar. Give them seriousness of life that the service in which they engage may be to their profit and spiritual good. Through their association with holy places and holy things, may they grow in the Christian life. And by their service in this earthly house where you manifest your glory, may they be prepared for that Mansion not made with hands, eternal in the heavens; through Jesus Christ our Lord. *Amen.*

CONTEMPORARY ACOLYTE PRAYER

Gracious God, the epitome of light and love: You call us to light the way for your people in a world of change and uncertainty. Grant to your acolytes reverent hearts, steady hands, and the will to persevere in service at your altar and at prayer. Bless and guide us by your wisdom and help us to spread your word throughout the world. Through Jesus Christ our lord, who lives and reigns with you and the Holy Spirit, one God now and forever. *Amen.*[1]

BEFORE THE SERVICE

Be present, Lord Jesus, be present! Grant that I may faithfully and loyally serve you in love and through my service proclaim, "In all things, God be glorified." *Amen.*[2]

AFTER THE SERVICE

Glory to you, Lord Jesus, Glory to you! Grant that as I have served in your presence, so I may witness faithfully and loyally to your love in the world and forever proclaim, "In all things, God be glorified." *Amen.*[3]

---

1. Ibid.

2. Dennis G. Michno, *A Manual for Acolytes: The Duties of the Server at Liturgical Celebrations* (Harrisburg, PA: Morehouse Publishing, 1981),11.

3. Ibid.